Rich Contractor Poor Contractor

How to become the Contractor everyone remembers and no one can resist

Mike Logan

Rich Contractor Poor Contractor How to become the Contractor everyone remembers and no one can resist

© 2017 Mike Logan

All rights reserved. No part of this book may be reproduced or transmitted in any form or by any means, electronic or mechanical, including photocopying and recording, or by any information storage and retrieval system, without permission in writing from the publisher.

This book is dedicated to all the honest,
hardworking contractors who are
striving for excellence and
fulfilling their dreams
of owning their own businesses.

Table of Contents

Introduction vi

Chapter 1: Trust Comes First 1

Chapter 2: Stand Out From the Crowd 13

Chapter 3: Perception is Reality 25

Chapter 4: Sales and Power 37

Chapter 5: Get Slightly Famous Locally 57

Chapter 6: Systematize Your Business 75

Chapter 7: Sub-Contractors 93

Chapter 8: There is a Gold Mine in Your Message 105

Chapter 9: The Power Marketing Program 133

Chapter 10: Strategic Messaging Formula 157

Introduction

I'm Mad as Hell, and I'm Not Going to Take It Anymore! — Howard Beale in Network (1976)

I remember the day well. It was August 15th, 2000. I was on my way to an appointment and I was going over in my mind as to what I was going to say and how I was going to give this sales presentation, as I usually do. I arrived about a half an hour early and I parked my car to go over some notes. As I parked, I happened to notice that a pickup truck in front of my appointments house with a competitor's sign on the door. This is quite common to see other pool companies on the same appointment that I'm on. I never liked it when they were there at the same time I was there, but after all, I was there early.

I waited for another 25 minutes. I then approached the house and rang the bell. The customer answered the door and I introduced myself. "Hi, I'm Mike Logan with Logan Pools." The customer told me, "I'm interviewing another pool company right now. Can you wait for about 15 minutes until were done? I'll come out and get you?" I reluctantly agreed, went back out to my car to wait. As I'm waiting, another car pulls up and parks in front of the pickup truck. I recognize the driver as a pool salesman from yet another pool company, and I'm thinking, "Great, this Yahoo has all three of us here at pretty much the same time."

I couldn't help but feel a little angry about this, but I swallowed my pride and waited for the 15 minutes, and sure enough, out comes the customer and also the other pool salesman that was being interviewed by him. Customer waves to me that it's my turn to come into the house, so I dutifully grab my catalog case and walk into the house and nod to the other salesman as he's walking by. I'm not feeling too good about this situation and neither is he. I'm feeling rather cheap. I get inside the house and greet the gentleman, try to be pleasant and proceed to do a warmup. However, I'm having trouble concentrating knowing that there's another salesman waiting behind me and there was one in front of me as I was coming in.

I didn't like the attitude of the client either. I'm sitting at the dining room table with him and we're talking about his project when he asked me, "How long is this going to take, because I've got another guy coming in in about 20 minutes?" Well, a thought came to mind. It was actually a line from a movie. The movie was Network, and it came out in 1976. In this movie, the character, Howard Beall has had enough, and he stands up and he yells, "I'm mad as hell and I'm not going to take this anymore." He further says, "I'm a human being and my life has value."

"I Don't Audition For Business!"

This line in the movie just consumed my thoughts, and I found myself being mad as hell and I decided, I'm not going to take this anymore. My life and my time has value as well. I stood up, looked the customer in the eye and told him, "It's obvious that you don't have much time, so I'm going to open up your schedule. I'm leaving right now." I packed up my case. As I'm walking out, he says, "Aren't you going to tell me how much this pool costs?" Biting my tongue and controlling my temper, I say, "No sir, I'm not going to do business with you. It's appears that you are interviewing several pool companies today and have scheduled them to be here at the same time. That is not respectful to me and the other salesmen. I don't work with people who don't respect my time. You have a good day."

From that moment on, I realized something. My current method of marketing and sales wasn't working. The old model just isn't working the way it used to work. All my competitors were selling the same way as me. We would get a phone call at the office with someone requesting an estimate on a swimming pool. We'd make an appointment, assign a salesman and out we go. That was pretty much all the qualifying that we did. All we needed to know was, "Are you interested in a pool?", and we would go out and spend our time trying to convince them to buy our pool. Our economy had been in a decline for the last 2 years and leads were hard to come by, so we did not disqualify too many potential buyers on the phone.

The Recession Was Here!

This was in 2008, and the recession was in full force. The clients had all the power, and they knew it. Business had come to a crawl because of the economy, and people were just not buying pools like they used to. And the ones who were buying pools were well aware that every pool salesman was very hungry and desperate to make a sale. The buyers were working both ends against the middle. They'd call out 5 and 6 different companies, work them against each other and get the lowest price and the best deal that they could get. In the meantime, all of us poor schmucks were just answering a cattle-call for free estimates. It's what I call auditioning to get business. I decided then and there, "I'm not going to do this anymore." I'm done with auditioning.

I need to find a better method of marketing and sales. I need to stand out from the crowd of these other pool companies competing for business the same way as I am. We all tend to start looking alike at that point. I need to figure out a way to differentiate myself from the crowd. I started on a journey. I was bound and determined to develop a brand new way of attracting and selling customers. I bought every marketing and sales book I could get my hands on that looked like it might have an answer. I scoured the internet looking for gurus that had different reports, programs, books, or materials that I could possibly gain some information from in an effort to devise a new marketing and sales system.

I spent thousands of dollars going to seminars, traveling thousands of miles all over the country to attend marketing and sales seminars. I paid to have breakfast and consult with Zig Ziglar (Secrets of Closing); I spent a week training with Joel Bauer (How to Persuade People Who Don't Want to Be Persuaded), I consulted with Ben Gay (The Closers), took three seminars with Brian Tracy (Professional Selling) and Tom Hopkin (Sales Boot Camp) and many, many, others. Most of them had great strategies and tactics that I was able to formulate into a new approach to my marketplace.

After attending dozens of seminars, reading over a hundred marketing and sales books, investing in different tapes, CD's and DVD programs I was able to create a polished powerful sales system.

Money Well Spent

I implemented this new sales system and it worked extremely well for a solid decade. I was the number one producer in my marketplace, and life was good. But around 2012, things began to change. The behavior of buyers was becoming different than it was a few years earlier. With the growth of social media and online review sites, buyers were all of a sudden equipped with unlimited information about swimming pools and could research various contractors prior to calling them for an estimate. Now the buyer did not need to have sales people to explain pros and cons of equipment or present the credentials of their companies. He could look it up online. The buyer has at his fingertips *Yelp, Google, You Tube, Instagram, Twitter* etc. **The buyer now had the power over a salesman, and he knew it.**

Once again it was necessary to design and create a new method of marketing and selling to address the "new buyer" of today.

It took me 2 years of research and testing, but once again I was able to design a profitable promotional system that works for today's sophisticated buyer. It's a new marketing and sales system that is drastically different from the one I developed with the Old Masters. I call it **Choreographed Persuasion**. I will touch upon it throughout this book.

One of the cornerstones of my system encompasses the importance of **establishing yourself as the #1 Expert or Trusted Advisor in your niche**. This book will give you a few ideas for accomplishing this. That's what this book is about. It's about giving you a roadmap where you can differentiate yourself from your competition. I'm in the swimming pool business, and so a lot of my examples are going to be geared toward that business, however the concepts, strategies, mechanisms and tactics that I present in this book applies to all niches, all trades, all professions.

Don't think, "Oh, I'm not in the swimming pool business, so this doesn't apply to me." These concepts apply to anyone and everyone who relies on marketing and sales to make a living. Your job, when you go through this book, is to look and see how you can apply these concepts to your business. What you don't want to do is to look at these concepts and say, "Ah, that won't apply to me.", or "That's old news", or "This won't work." There's no profit in that.

Maybe all the strategies won't work for your business, but I guarantee you, most of these will if you just give them a try. Be positive about it.

Read this book as if you're looking for nuggets of gold, and you will find them.

1

Trust Comes First

This is the business we have chosen
Hymen Roth in The Godfather: Part II (1974)

If you're a contractor, you probably became one for the same reasons that I did, some twenty years ago. You've learned your craft by working for other contractors for a number of years. I worked for eighteen years for three or four different firms learning my craft in the swimming pool industry. For eighteen years I learned about designing pools, excavation of pools, rebar, gunite, plumbing, decking, tile, plaster, waterfalls, and on, and on, and on. I learned my craft well. I learned how to design and build beautiful swimming pools.

One day I decided that I knew more than the boss. I was tired of management not seeing things the way I see them, and so I said, "Hey, I've got to start my own company, and let's do this right." That's what I did, and I bet that's what you did too. You learned your craft and then you went out, studied and you passed the contractor's test, then you got your license. Now you are a contractor. You opened the door to your business, maybe you worked out of your home at first or rented a mall office. You called the Yellow Page company and got an ad in the Yellow Pages, got some business cards printed up, maybe had a contract worked up by a lawyer, and you were ready to go.

Do You Know the Business of Contracting?

You probably struggled for a while getting some traction in the marketplace, but soon you were making sales, and you were building your products. As you were going along, you probably realized something. There's a lot more to being a contractor, and being in business all by yourself than working for somebody else. You suddenly realized it's not enough to know how to build the product that your selling. You now have to learn how to run a business. Suddenly you have to be an expert at marketing, sales, employee supervision, bookkeeping, payroll, legal issues, etc. You spend years learning how to construct the item that you are contracting for, but you didn't spend much time learning the business end of being a contractor. That's why ninety-five percent of all new contracting businesses fail within the first five years.

A lot of people say it's because they were undercapitalized. They didn't start with enough money to begin with. In many cases that's probably true. However, I think the biggest cause of failure with new contractors is they fail to learn the business of contracting. If you don't know the business aspects such as budgeting, payroll, book keeping, marketing, sales and such, you're doomed for failure. I know I struggled when I first began as a contractor over twenty years ago. I was very fortunate when I started my business, it was during a boom time. It was very easy to make sales. I had enough cash flow to make up for the mistakes I made on the business end.

Let me tell you what this book is about and what it's not about. I want to hit upon a couple of very important things about being a contractor. This book is not an exhaustive study on contracting, rather it's a short introduction aimed at awakening contractors as to what is happening in today's marketplace, and what they must do to not only survive but dominate in their markets.

Become The # 1 Choice in Your Marketplace

It's not going to be about how to handle accounting, how to do budgeting, how to supervise employees. It's not about the day to day operations of the business, but rather I wanted to touch upon the marketplace and how you need to adjust your marketing and sales efforts to match the challenges of today's economy.

You see, as a contractor, you have two strikes against you in the general populations opinion of you. That's because you're a contractor which is one of the least respected professions. Contractors are right behind lawyers, as far as being trustworthy, honest, and respected. Right away, just by the nature of the business you're in, people are very skeptical about doing business with you. Actually, let me rephrase that. Most people are afraid to do business with you. It's because they either have been ripped off by a contractor or they know people who have been lied to or ripped off, and possibly lost thousands of dollars in the past.

It's Not Your Fault, But You're Guilty Anyway

Now you might be the most honest man on the face of the earth in your eyes, but you're still a contractor. You are guilty by association. If you're going to overcome this fear in the customer's eyes, you need to do some very important. You need to change the customer's perception of you. Your job is not to become an expert in marketing and sales, that comes down the road. Your number one job at the very onset is to show your customers that you are responsible, that you are honest, and that you're not a crook.

Before you start pitching how great your product is, and all the benefits and the features of it, you need to develop a strategy and a plan to convey to the general public that you are truthful and can be trusted. If you do that first, the sales will come much easier than if you're just perceived as another contractor.

Positioning Yourself as a Leader

Your first order of business is to determine how can you position yourself in the customer's eyes as being the most trustworthy contractor that they could possibly do business with. That is what this chapter and most of this book is all about. You probably noticed that this book is rather short. It is short by design. I've written two other books, both of them about two hundred pages long. I then subsequently read some studies about people's habits of reading business books. A statistic stuck out in my mind as quite alarming. Eighty-five percent of all people who buy business books will not get past the first one hundred pages. Most people buy business books and they lose interest in them before they get through half of the book. That's why this book is short. I want to get to the point. I want to drive home a message to all contractors, important information that could make the difference whether or not you stay in business or go bankrupt.

The goal of my book is not to make money. If it was, I would not offer this book for such a low price on Kindle. I want to pay if forward if you will, because I love the contracting business, specifically swimming pool contracting. It's been very good to me. I've seen a lot of fellow contractors over the years struggle and go out of business unnecessarily. They just didn't know what to focus on to thrive in the marketplace. Most of the contractors think if they just build their product just a little bit better than the competition business will come their way. If you're a roofer, you use materials just a little bit better than what the average contractor does, and then you brag about it to your clients. If you're a swimming pool contractor, you think if you just put more rebar in the pool, make their gunite a little bit thicker, that's going to put you head and shoulders above the competition, and get you more sales.

Time for a Reality Check

Well, I hate to be the bearer of bad news, but improving your product just a little bit better than the competition is short lived. Oh, you might make a couple of sales here and there, because you have improved the product, but it won't take long for the competition to figure out what you're doing, and they'll match it, or perhaps even go beyond it, and make it better. That's not the issue with your customers. You see, your customers most likely view all contractors as being alike. They view the products that you offering pretty much alike. They see that you could all build things pretty much equally. If the customer assumes that all contractors are pretty much the same they will most likely choose the one with the lowest price. The main thing that's going to separate you from the competition and influence the buyer the most is not how good your product is but how trustworthy you are

That is the major determining factor in a client's mind as to whom they're going to choose. Who do they trust the most? Then they will get into the product details. Then they get into the features and benefits. Trustworthiness trumps all else. The contractor who is seen as the most honest and trustworthy will get the lion's share of the business. That's what we're going to cover in subsequent chapters.

Rich Contractors ... develop strategies and tactics that position themselves as trustworthy, reliable and different.

Poor Contractors ... focus on features, benefits, and having a better product.

2

Stand Out
from the Crowd

I'm Kind of a Big Thing

Ron Burgundy in Anchorman: The Legend of Ron Burgundy (2004)

Quit trying to be *better* than your competition and start figuring out how you can be not only better than, but also **different** from them! You see, most business owners are trying to figure out exactly how to produce better products, provide better service, present better features, and — the worst of all — they're trying to price all of this at a lower cost. Creating better products or services are worthwhile goals, but the problem is that coming up with a better product or service isn't easy. Often your clients won't take the time to determine the subtle **differences** that make your product or your service significantly better than your competitor's. Customers won't spend the time and energy trying to figure what just what makes you different.

Being a little better than the competition is not the same as being different from the competition.

Being different is where the profit is found. Instead of trying to be better than or somewhat like the competition, you must build a strategy that simply declares that your company is definably unique from the competition.

Be A Detective…Snoop On Competition

Now, how do you go about doing this? Well, one way is to go to each of your competitors' websites and look at their "About" pages. Read through the some of the descriptions and note the highlights of some of their common themes. They're probably listing remarks such as, "Great customer service. We've been in business 100 years. You've tried the rest, now try the best," etc. Now, look and compare four of five of these type of comments on a competitor's page with the ones on the "About" page of your website. Does your "About" page look very similar to those of your competitors or does it stand out distinctly from them?

This is a really good way to see areas in which you're already different, and those where you are the same.

How do you go about discovering by what means you can be not merely different but unique from your competition? In other words, what makes you the best choice among your competitors? What are your strengths? One way is to ask your previous customers. I would advise that you pick ten to fifteen of your customers and either ask them some questions or give them a short survey to fill out. The number one question I would ask is, "Why did you choose us in the first place?" In other words, "What attracted you to our business? Why did you choose us? Having done business with us, what did we do that the others didn't do or didn't offer you? What could we have performed better?"

Unique Selling Proposition

You see, every company must develop a unique value proposition, or some people call it "Unique

Selling Proposition. A USP differentiates your company from other companies' products and services. Often this is called "Competitive Advantage". Your ability to create a brand and maintain it in a competitive marketplace can make or break your business. Just look at some of the most successful companies in the world. They all have a very clear and distinct brand. Coca Cola, Federal Express, Apple etc. You must create a distinct brand for your company. Your customers are bombarded every day with messages that are saying, "Buy me. Buy me." The value of a brand is that it can help the customer choose the best product or Contractor from all the possible choices.

A brand suggests value, quality, scarcity or reliability. A brand helps you cut through the competitive cluster and get customers' attention and make the sale. A brand is credibility and guarantee the customer will be satisfied and get what she or he is paying for. A brand represents the promise that you make to get the sale, and the promises you keep after you get the sale. Both are important, but having satisfied and happy clients is the secret to long-term business success. It's the key to getting repeat business and referrals.

You must keep your promises. The most valuable asset in both your business and personal life is your great reputation. Your reputation is what people say about you when you are not there. It's how they describe your products and services after they have purchased and used them. Your reputation is how you are known to your customers. **Every customer contact with your company either builds up or tears down your reputation.** You must put a system in place that manages your reputation on a day by day basis. This can't be left to chance. It's mission critical to your success especially with the advent of the Internet. Your reputation is online 24/7 for everybody to see. Research shows that 85% of people looking for a Contractor will first search for online reviews prior to contacting them.

Having numerous 5-star reviews online can be a powerful differentiator from your competitors. If a potential customer sees that your company has 20 or more 5-star reviews and your competitors only have 2 or 3 who do you think they will call first? What company do you think they will perceive as more trustworthy? You must establish an ongoing system for generating great reviews online from your clients.

To illustrate my point, stop reading this and get on Google and let's take a look at your company's reputation. You can search for any company by name plus the city and it reveals their reputation. Once you do this you will see that the first line is your company's website. The second line usually says something about the company and the third line shows your reputation. What did you find about your company? Do you have a 5-star rating? Do you have any bad reviews? I also recommend checking out each of your competitors' online reputation. Also check with Yelp and Google+.

After making a sales presentation have you ever had the customer say "I have to think about it"? Picture this, you make the same sales presentation but this time there is the customer's neighbor, friend or a relative present. The relative or friend says to your customer "You really should do business with this company. They're amazing! They do great work and are reliable!" Would you get the sale then? I'll let you in on a little secret. The *Neilson Global Trust in Advertising* did a survey Q3 2011. The survey asked "What extent do you trust the following forms of advertising?

Biggest Shift in marketing in 10 years.

92% responded that they trust "recommendations from people we know- a referral," and "consumer opinions posted online" came in second at 72%! That means that three out of four people trust online reviews almost as much as a personal recommendation from a friend. This is huge! Can you see now why it is mission critical to have a great reputation online?

A great 5-star online reputation gives your company a tremendous competitive advantage. Before you attempt any other form of marketing you should establish a rock solid reputation online.

The majority of sales people and companies today ignore this very important strategy. The fail to identify and articulate what separates them from their competition. If your competition is not paying attention to this, you can take advantage and leap head and shoulders ahead of them. If you can answer satisfactorily the following question, you will dominate and own the marketplace: Why should I choose you or your company over all the other choices that I have available? Answering this question is mission critical to your company's success.

Jack Welch, former CEO of General Electric, said, "If you don't have a competitive advantage, don't compete." Therefore, you must determine a great response to this question. Why should they do business with you over your competition? Answer that question and the marketplace is yours.

Rich Contractors ... set themselves and their company apart from the competition by being not only better but different.

Poor Contractors ... try to be better instead of being different from the competition.

3

Perception is Reality

What we've got here is failure to communicate
Strother Martin in Cool Hand Luke (1967)

Are you baffled when you lose a sale to a competitor? Especially if that competitor does terrible work, has a bad reputation, and you know that your company is so much better than that company. Does it leave you perplexed and wondering, "how could this happen?" How can you lose to such a terrible competitor? Worse yet, they bought from another Contractor and did not even give you a call to bid on the job. Well, it's probably because your advertising and marketing is ineffective

Chances are your advertising and marketing is not informing the public how you are different from all the other choices and what major benefits they will receive if they do business with you. Most companies, when they advertise, use the same bunch of platitudes that all the other companies are using such as: we do high-quality work; we've been in business for

25 years; our craftsmen are the best. You see, these phrases are what we call platitudes and platitudes make your marketing message dull and common place. Let me give you a definition of what a platitude is as it pertains to marketing. Platitudes are words or phrases that are dull, obvious, or predictable that lack power to create interest because they're overused and unoriginal, that are nevertheless still commonly used as though they were unique or distinctive.

Useless Claims of Competence

Let me give you a couple of more examples of platitudes that you're probably using in your advertising. Are you putting any of the following in your advertising?

- We offer the best service
- We have the largest selection
- We do the job right the first time
- You've tried the rest, now try the best
- We're number 1
- We use state-of-the-art equipment

Does any of the above sound familiar? I bet it does. You've heard this kind of junk for years, but let me ask you this, do you have these terms in your marketing? I bet you do. In fact, why don't you take a look at your advertising and marketing and see if it's loaded with platitudes.

Here's the bottom line. These commonly used phrases fill up your marketing and advertising and they're hurting your profits. They're destroying your client attraction opportunities. You see, these platitudes don't distinguish or separate you in the marketplace. They don't quantify or specify anything. They're not believable. They usually are not provable and they cause your prospects to minimize, discount, disbelieve, or worst of all, ignore you altogether. Ultimately what happens is your target market ends up believing that you and your business are just like everybody else in your industry. And if that's the case they may as well select the contractor with the lowest proposal.

Differentiate or Die…Jack Trout

It's not how much better you think you are than your competitors that matters. It's what the public thinks about you that matters. Their perception is reality to them whether or not it's true. They will think you are no different because you have introduced yourself to the marketplace as just one more contractor looking for work in a whole sea of contractors looking for work. You're being perceived to be just like everybody else and the real message that you're portraying to your market is, "Hey, me, too! I'm a contractor. I do this work, too." You see, this is one factor as to why you're not dominating your market. This is why your sales and revenues are dependent upon the force of the market and not your ability to win over more and more customers. You're not communicating to the general public just who you are, specifically why they should do business with you and nobody else. That's called a lack of communication.

If you are looking to hire a Roofing Contractor, and you notice a Yellow Page ad that says, "We'll find that leak in your roof and we will fix it." "Well, I would hope so" is going through the mind of the person reading that ad. How about, "We'll do it right the first time?" Well, again, I would hope that you would do it right the first time.

So, you see, claims like that mean nothing in the marketplace. Everybody says those things, and if you're saying them too, you're all lumped in into one category: Contractors. If you're all the same, the customer says in his mind, "Well, I'll just go with the lowest price. They're all the same. They all say they do quality work. They've all been in business for a long time. They all say they stand by their work. They all say they do it right the first time. So, I'll just get the lowest price." That's one reason why you're losing business. I'll address more reasons later on in this book.

Your Message Must Get Noticed.

What you need to do is communicate in your advertising and your marketing how you are different from your competition and the difference must be something valuable to your potential clients. If you want to stand out from the competition, you must innovate with your marketing efforts. You must create specific and strategic marketing headlines, messages, and campaigns that absolutely separate you from your competitors and cause your prospects to look at you different than your competitors.

You want them to think "hey, this company is totally different from the other ads I've been seeing". Saying how long you've been in business in your ad has minimal effect. Nobody cares about how long you've been in business until they realize what you can do for them and how much you care about them. You need to communicate just who you are to your prospective clients, but there's a big problem. We live in an over-communicated society right now. Communicating is very difficult because we are bombarded with thousands of advertisements daily with thousands of marketing messages. There's just too much noise out there. You have to figure a way to be seen and be heard above the noise.

You need to position yourself in the mind of your prospective clients as the only logical choice for their need. Positioning is a mind game and you need to learn how to play the game.

According to the Chamber of Commerce ninety-five percent of new Contracting businesses fail within the first five years of operation. If you have made it past the five-year mark congratulations! But don't get too comfortable just yet. Ask yourself, is it getting harder and harder to make sales? Are there more competitors now than five years ago? Have I lowered my prices in order to compete? Is my marketing working like it did a couple of years ago or has it lost its impact?

Old Marketing Strategies Don't Work Today

Today's marketplace is no longer responsive to the strategies that worked in the past. There are just too many products. There's too many companies and there's too much marketing noise. In all your marketing pieces, you must appear different from the competition.

On your website, on your brochures, on your business card, on Facebook, on your mailers, and everything you do to market you company, you must appear different than the competition or they will link you in with every other contractor out there. Jack Trout said it best "Differentiate or Die". Before people will do business with you, they must know who you are, they must like you, and they must trust you.

Rich Contractors ... look differently, act differently, sell differently, and market differently!

Poor Contractors ... all look, act, sell, and market the same.

In the next chapter, we're going to cover strategies for becoming the number one go-to contractor in your marketplace. We're going to show you strategies and tactics for you to be known, liked, and trusted head and shoulders above any other contractor competing for your business.

4

Sales and Power

Take Back the Power, and the Sale is Yours!

Mike Logan

I started my sales career in 1976. I went to work for a swimming pool contractor as a designer/salesman. Being new to the field of sales, I made it a point to educate myself on how to be a good salesman. I bought books, and at that time cassette tape programs, went to several seminars to learn how to sell. I studied under sales trainers like Tom Hopkins, Brian Tracy, and Zig Ziglar to name a few.

I received some very valuable information at that time on how to sell. The information I got from those people at that time was tremendous and it made me quite successful for a while. The sales techniques that I learned from those type of sales trainers worked in the 70s, in the 80s, and in the early 90s, but they don't work today.

Selling has dramatically changed in the economy that we live in today. Many people call it the new economy. You have to ask yourself, "Do consumers today buy the same way today as they did 10, 20, or 30 years ago?

Most of you would probably agree, they buy differently today. Why? Why has the consumer gone through a change that makes him think differently how he makes purchases? You see, 20 years ago, there was a bridge between companies and the consumers, and that bridge was the salesmen. Companies would send out sales people to meet with the clients and go over all the benefits and features of their products. 10, 20, 30 years ago and more, that's how people learned about products. It was from the sales person.

The sales person was the important gap between the consumer and the companies that they were representing. There was an education process that took place between the salesmen and the consumer.

We live in a completely different era right now and the consumer knows all about our products, our company and possibly our sales people. They know what services you offer. They know about your competitors. They know how long you've been in business. They know everything about you simply by doing a Google search on their phone or on their computer.

The Internet Has Given Them Power

Because of this power, consumers no longer willing to be manipulated by pushy sales people because they know they have many other options and choices to choose from. As an example, if a consumer is looking to get a new roof put on their house, they go online and they can research unlimited roofing contractors and new business in their area.

They can go on their websites and learn all about each and every company. They can review the products and the services that each company offers. They can go on sites like Yelp and Google+ and check out their reputation. All this they can do prior to having a sales rep from your company come out and talk to them about their roof.

Because the consumer is armed with all this information, sales people have to be very careful how they go about their sales process because now if you try the old sales techniques such as" Always be Closing", trying to get the consumer to answer several questions that result in the yes answer and so on. You're going to come across as being a manipulative, pushy salesman.

You're going to be seen like the proverbial used car salesman and they're not going to relate to you, and you're not going to make a sale. Most consumers will think you have an ulterior motive when you show up anyway, that you're out there to manipulate them and push them into buying something they don't really want.

This is what you're going up against every time you're on a sales call in this economy. The customer today will not put up with a pushy salesperson because **Consumers Have Many Choices and They Know It.**

They have the power to go elsewhere. They have the information at their fingertips to look for another vendor should they not like you or what you're offering or how you are trying to manipulate them into a sale.

Why is it that most salespeople today are still using the old way of selling, still using the old sales techniques of the 60s, 70s and 80s? Why are they doing that? Well, many of the sales trainers that have guided the way to modern day sales training are still around, and they're still selling the way they did way back when.

We have people like Tom Hopkins still putting on seminars with his guide to greatness in sales. We've got Brian Tracey still doing sale seminars, and he's been selling books and sales training programs for 40 years.

You've got Jeffrey Gitmer's *Sales Bible*. Zig Ziglar's materials on skill selling is still out there even though he's passed away; his corporation is still conducting sales seminars, and the methods and strategies and the tactics that they're teaching in these seminars are the same ones they've been teaching for 40 years!

I have nothing against these older gurus who are still selling the way they have for many years. They were wonderful people. I learned a lot from these men. However, the consumer today doesn't respond to these sales strategies. In fact, they're repelled by them. If you try to do most of what is being taught today with the average consumer, they will probably show you the door.

Another thing happens when consumers feel like they've been manipulated and pushed into a sale, they will go online and leave bad reviews about you and your company on Yelp. They will also go to Twitter and LinkedIn and tell all their friends about you. Pretty soon, you can't sell.

Death of a Salesman

When I think of the old sales techniques, it reminds me of Arthur Miller's play, Death of a Salesman. In the play, the character Willy Loman is an elderly salesman still out in the field using his old sales techniques, and they're not working. He tries everything he knows to make sales, but the problem is that everything he knows is outdated and doesn't work anymore. He doesn't know how to adjust to the new consumer. That's quite similar to sales people today who are still using the old techniques.

The old strategies and tactics are not working and they should be stopped. New techniques and tactics, and strategies need to be applied. You must realize that if you continue to use the same old sales tactic that you've always used, you'll never experience great success and selling. You'll always have the mediocre results that you have right now.

Don't Act, Look, or Talk Like a Salesman

In today's business environment, the consumer appears to have all the power because he has at his fingertips unlimited information about the product and the contractors he's planning on doing business with. The key to selling is to regain that power back from the customer. We need to take control of the sales environment and control the customer's buying behavior. One thing that is imperative in this process is that we cannot be perceived as salesmen. Salesmen don't have the power today. If you're perceived as a salesman, you'll be treated like every other competitor who is trying to make a sale. You'll be treated like a salesman.

In the swimming pool business, you, as well as four or five of your competitors, will go out on sales calls to the customer's home and be interviewed by the customer. It's an audition type scenario. You don't want to compete in this type of a sales scenario. You don't have any control at that point. The consumer does. The last thing you ever want to look like is another salesman. As an example, when people go to the department store and the sales clerk asks them, "May I help you?" what's the first thing the customer says? "No, thanks, just looking." In other words, "Get away from me, salesman. I don't want to be sold." Also, if you go to a car lot and you're just looking for various cars and out comes the salesperson, it's the same thing. He'll say, "Hey, what can I help you with today?" The customer says, "Just looking. Don't need any help." His or her guard is up.

People just don't want to deal with salespeople, so you cannot be seen as just another salesperson. Therefore, we can't look like salespeople. We can't act like salespeople and we certainly can't talk like salespeople. We can't do the things that salespeople do that will immediately identify them to everybody else as a salesperson. You will lose the power. You gain power by not being another salesperson. For you to have the power, it depends on three things:

1. Authority

2. Celebrity

3. Exclusivity

Now what am I talking about with authority? If you establish yourself as an authority in your field, you are looked at as the expert or industry leader more than just another salesman. As discussed in previous chapters, you need to achieve authority status. That's the number one thing that you can do to separate yourself as being seen as a salesman. If you become an authority, you are now the expert, not the salesman. Also, if you happen to achieve a status of being locally famous and well-known in your marketplace it will position you as a local celebrity. This also separates you from the salesman's class.

Be A Specialist

Third, if you want to separate yourself from just being another salesman, you need to specialize in a certain type of product. For instance, in the swimming pool industry, swimming pool salesmen typically will sell any kind of pool that the customers want. Doesn't matter what size, shape or type. They're salesmen and it's their job to make a sale. They don't take the time to determine what will be best for the customer, they just want to make a quick sale. Very often this lack of concern for the buyer is so apparent that the customer feels like he is being sold and puts up his guard. You immediately come across as just another salesperson. I determined long ago that I wanted to become a Specialist and not a General Practitioner. I wanted to be more like the Cardiologist that you had to wait in line to get an appointment with than the run of the mill Doctor. I wanted to be selective and only do business with people who wanted a high quality pool and were willing to pay top dollar. I realized that I needed to position myself as the Expert and Authority on high end custom swimming pools in my marketplace.

I developed a reputation for building pools that when you walk into the back yard for the first time, your jaw drops, and you say, "Wow! Who built this? I've got to have one of these." I've heard it said that my company is the Mercedes Benz of the pool companies in the area. I don't project an arrogant attitude in my marketing, but, at the same time, people know that my pools cost more because they are designed and built to a high standard. I've also made it somewhat difficult to get an appointment with me. I charge for my design work and estimates even though every one of my competitors do it for free. That's the kind of exclusivity I've established. I've also written books, articles, blogs and I've created and syndicated several videos out on to the Internet. These are videos about pool ownership and tips for consumers, not so much about me. It took a lot of work and planning, but I've established myself locally as an authority. I speak at local Chamber of Commerce events, and I sponsor Little League, Soccer, and Basketball teams. I am well-known in the area so I'm a local celebrity.

Become Famous...Locally

Once you achieve the status of being an authority and or a local celebrity and you specialize in a certain niche, you then become unique. You're different than the pack of salespeople that are out there at which point you now have the power. The customer should not perceive you as just another salesman because you have set yourself apart in such a manner that he now perceives you as someone who is a professional. You are now no longer a commodity. You are a specialist.

This principle works across all professions. Take, for example, the medical field. At the bottom of the rung, we have the general practitioners. These are just your everyday doctors that you would go to see for a regular check-up. Let's say you go to your doctor with a complaint of chest pains, and he does a diagnosis on you and says, "You've got a heart problem. You need to go see a cardiac specialist, I'm just a generalist." T

he next thing you will do is grab your phone, call that cardiac doctor's office, and ask for an appointment. You will be informed that he's booked up, and you can't get an appointment for several weeks. You have to wait to see this specialist because he's unique and in demand. He's not like the general doctor. You could get an appointment with a doctor in twenty-four hours, but with the specialist it's going to take you two, three, four, or sometimes five weeks to get an appointment. He's in demand. People wait to see a specialist.

After you finally get to see the specialist, he's going to do some diagnostic testing on you to determine what you need. He then will talk to you and tell you exactly what you should do and what kind of treatment you should have, what kind of medications you should have. With specialists, patients will not question their advice. If he says, "We have to do this," you do it.

If you are seen as a specialist and an authority, you will command the same respect. Customers will listen to you and follow your recommendations.

Specialists Diagnose Before Prescribing a Solution

When you meet with your clients, you should spend a good amount of time doing a diagnosis as to what they actually need and what would be best for them. After the diagnosis, then you can make some recommendations just as the specialist does.

Now, at this point, if you've established yourself as the expert in your field, customers will listen to you and take your advice without questioning it. If you're perceived as just another salesman, customers will question everything you say because they don't trust you. People don't trust salespeople. People do trust experts and authority figures. That's who you want to become, the expert in your field. Once you are the Expert you are in control of the sales process. Clients will come to you rather than you chasing them and "auditioning" for their business. You set the price and terms of doing business with you, not the client. Other professionals such as Lawyers, Doctors and Architects determine what they are worth why not you. It's time you took control and take back the power from the consumer. Life is so much better when you call the shots.

Rich Contractors ... are seen as
Experts, Celebrities, and Trusted Advisors

Poor Contractors ... are seen as
Pushy Sales People

5

Get Slightly Famous Locally

> **It took me fifteen years to discover I had no talent for writing, but I couldn't give it up because by that time I was too famous.**
> *Robert Benchley*

Most contractors struggle to keep the cash register ringing and the work flowing. They advertise. The send out mailings. They make cold calls. They stay up at night worrying whether they'll have enough money to meet payroll. There are a few contractors that seemingly have all the business they can handle, and then some. Potential customers line up to buy from them, often waiting months until they can be sold. So strong is the customer's desire to buy from these particular contractors, that they'll wait, and wait, and pay top dollar, even though other contractors are available now, and are eager to take their business, and possibly charge must less.

Why are some contractors busy and in demand virtually all the time, while others struggle to get by? One reason might be because they have established themselves as the leaders in their field. The top plumber, photographer, architect, accountant, pool contractor, lawyer, doctor, consultant, and so on, all appear to be the top dog in their industry. They are in short the top thought leader in their industry. They're considered so knowledgeable, and expert in their field, that customers flock to them, while their competitors wonder why, and must settle for picking up the leftovers. As top dogs in their profession, they have gained guru status through self-promotion and publicity. Top dog contractors are recognized authorities in their field, and, because of this elevated status as the industry leader, they enjoy greater visibility and reputation than their counterparts, not to mention more income and wealth.

Self-Promotion and Publicity Is Mission Critical!

They are not gurus because they are more talented, or successful, or because their performance and track record are superior to yours. Instead they've gained this status through self-promotion and publicity. They are top dogs, not because they are great at what they do, but because they are great at selling and marketing themselves and what they do. Have you ever looked at some of these contractors who are known as leaders in their fields, and thought, "How did they become that way? Why does the news media and the public fawn all over these guys?" Have you ever felt that you know more than they do and y that you build a better product than they do? Well, you too can join them with expert status. You just need to get a deliberate plan of self-promotion.

Once you become a recognized leader in your field, and are seen as an expert, and the top dog, you will enjoy more success with less advertising, and marketing than you've ever experienced. Much has been written about selling and marketing for contractors. There's one marketing strategy that if you master it, eliminates the need to do most of the other types of selling and marketing. That is becoming a guru.

Once you become a guru in your field, you can do less advertising, less marketing, and the people will come to you, rather than you chasing them down.

Once you've achieved the expert status, many people are predisposed to buy from you, and won't even consider the competition. Since you're in demand, you don't negotiate your prices; your prices can remain whatever you want them to be. The greater your status as an expert in the field, the less likely that your clients are going to question your work, your advice, or your judgement.

You Won't Audition Ever Again!

You can accept and select only the jobs that interest you, and only the ones that you want to work on. You can hand pick your clients, and eliminate the ones you don't want to work with. All because you are the expert in your field. How do you go about establishing yourself as the leader in your field? Well first of all, you don't have to become the nationally known leader in the field, just locally. You just have to be slightly famous within your marketing territory. There's several ways you can do that. It's going to take a little work, and a little bit of effort, but it'll be well worth it. Here are a few areas that you can focus on to become the leader in your local niche.

Become an Author

Number one, writing articles for publications is the quickest and easiest way. It's usually the first step at building up your reputation locally. Writing articles that you can get published in local newspapers and magazines is a great self-promotion strategy. Now when you write these articles, you're not writing them about you or your company. Pretty much you're giving tips to the general population about your particular product, or niche. For instance, if you're a roofing contractor, you might write articles on topics such as: When Do You Need a New Roof, What You Should Know About Your Roof; How to Select the Best Materials for Your New Roof; How to Find a Reputable Roofing Contractor; A Consumers' Guide to Roofing.

You do not write about yourself and all the awards you've won. This is intended to help your potential client. You're giving him information that he can use, thereby establishing you as an expert. Probably the best thing you can do to establish yourself as an industry leader is to write a book. Now I know that sounds like a really huge undertaking, but, in this electronic age with "print on demand" book services such as Amazon's Create Space, you can write an eBook and have it published online within days of writing it. Thereby establishing you as a recognized author. People look at authors automatically as an expert in that field. There's lots of how to books on the market on how to write an eBook. I would suggest that you definitely look into writing a short eBook, getting it up on line for sale, perhaps on Amazon. This will no doubt propel you to the expert status that you're looking to gain in your marketplace.

You then can advertise on your website your book, maybe give it away for free for people who opt in on your website, giving you their email, name, and address perhaps. It's a fantastic giveaway, and a great way to build a list. Another way to establish yourself as the leader in your field, in your niche is to give speeches locally. Check with the local Chamber of Commerce to make yourself available to speak before local business groups. It could be just a short twenty-minute presentation on your particular niche. The Chamber of Commerce is always looking for speakers. This is a great way to network at the Chamber functions, and established yourself as an expert in your area at the same time.

Your Website Is Your Most Powerful Marketing Tool

What is the one thing that a sales person or business owner should have before talking to new prospects? What's the first and most important sales tool that you have available? When I ask various business people and salesman this question, many times, they come back with, "A business card." I say, "No. It's not a business card." Before you get your business cards printed up, you should have a website.

In developing your website, obviously, you have to get a domain name setup. Make sure your domain name is simple. It could be your company name or it could be the industry that you're in if you can get that .com. Keep your websites name simple. Furthermore, a one or two-page website is typically all that's necessary for contractors. A lot of companies have been building really elaborate websites for a long time and it seems that people just don't take the time to read all those pages and information. It should be just long enough to make them want to contact you.

Now, just because it's a simple website, it doesn't mean that you shouldn't pay a lot of attention on its development. One thing you don't want to do is have your cousin or brother-in-law do the webpage. You want a professional. You need actually two professionals. You need a web designer who could actually put it together and up online. But more importantly, you need a marketing expert to develop a strategy for your website.

Don't be concerned so much with the beauty of the website. You want to be concerned with the purpose and effectiveness of the website. The purpose of any website for a contractor is to facilitate the customers buying decision. Your websites should move them along the buying process and get them to make a decision based on what you have said in your website.

You should ask yourself 3 questions when developing your website.

The **first question** is what action would you like your customers and prospects to take when visiting your website? In other words, what do you want them to do when they look at your website? Do you want them to call you, contact you? Do you want them to watch a video or read an article? Do you want them to download a report? What is it that you want them to do? It's very critical that you know this because that is part of the strategy that will be developed for your website. The key here is to focus on action, not information. What action do you want your visitors to take?

The **second question** you should ask when developing your website is what would you like your customers and prospects to learn when visiting your website? Do you want them for instance to learn about your company? Do you want them to learn why you're better than your competition? Do you want them to learn how your products work or do you want them to watch your sales video? On this question, you're focusing on information.

Videos Grab Viewers Attention. To convey this information, video is probably the most effective tool on a website. People today don't want to read long copy on websites. They are conditioned to turn the channel with their remote control while watching TV. If they are not interested in one show, just click, they go to the next one. It's the same with the website, so video really captures the viewers' attention. If you can, try to have videos created and placed on your website giving the prospects the information that they are looking for rather than long drawn out text.

The **third and final question** you should ask yourself before developing your website is what are the reasons your customers and prospects visit your website? What are they looking for? What do they want to do or find when they get to your website? Do they want to find your phone number? Do they want directions to your office? Are they looking for research about your company or learn about your product? Are they responding to an ad you placed in the newspaper? You need to find out what the typical client is looking for when they come to your website.

Remember, to have an effective website, one that produces results, you need to have a marketing expert that can formulate the strategies and the content of your website to maximize client attraction and lead conversions. Secondly and less important than the first is a competent webmaster to put it all together. The webmaster is not designing any of the content or strategies, just pretty much putting it all together from how the marketing expert has directed. Remember, you're not going for pretty, you're going for effective. Don't skimp on the most powerful marketing tool you have, your website. Look for two professionals, the marketing strategists and the webmaster to develop your website.

Websites today are not optional. You must have a viable website. In developing your website, you want to make sure it is chock filled with valuable information for your potential clients. A great way to gain exposure is to make videos and post them on YouTube and various video sites. These videos would be mainly comprised of frequently asked questions in your particular fields. Again, you want to give information, not do self-promotion. The more the videos, articles, and books you have out in the marketplace, the more you are going to appear to be the industry leader.

The marketplace loves the expert in the field. You already have the knowledge that you need to be an expert in your field. Now you need to promote yourself in such a manner that the general public will see you as the number one go to contractor, because everywhere they look, you are there. You were on the internet. You were on YouTube. You've written books, articles, Ezines. You have given speeches at local functions. Perhaps you could also sponsor local sports teams. Put your ads in the high school yearbooks. Make sure that you are seen everywhere. You build yourself up in your reputation as an expert by giving your knowledge away in a variety of forums, articles, books, seminars, speeches, newsletter, Ezines, websites, and videos. Just make sure that they're all done in a professional manner, nothing cheesy, and you're giving away valuable information, and you're not bragging about yourself.

If You Build It, They Will Come to You

Once you become the local expert in your niche, people will find a way to your door, and they come to you for your business, you're not going to them. When this occurs, you name your prices, your terms, and do business the way you want to do. When you're just running regular ads as the next contractor out there, people see you as a commodity, and nothing special, and then they will work you over with other contractors, try to squeeze out the lowest bid they can, giving you the least amount of profit, and making you do the most amount of work. Once you are the expert in your field, you now have the power, not the buyer.

Take the time to develop this reputation in your marketplace. It might take a little while, but it'll pay off ten times or more, from the amount of time, and investment that you made. Become the thought leader, and own the marketplace.

Rich Contractors … become slightly famous and are seen as Trusted Experts.

Poor Contractors … continue to be seen by customers as just another contractor out to get their money.

6

Systematize Your Business

Expect the best, plan for the worst, and prepare to be surprised.
Denis Waitley

Ryan and Sheryl had dreamed of putting in a custom swimming pool for years. They often talked about the type of pool that they would like to have and what it would look like. They wanted a pool that reminded them of their trip to Maui. They wanted a free form pool, with a raised spa, rock waterfall, and tropical landscaping that would remind them of their recent trips to Hawaii. They knew exactly what they wanted on their dream pool and now finally, they were ready to make it happen.

Ryan and Sheryl were very careful of selecting a swimming pool builder because they knew it was very important to get the right one. They had heard a lot of stories about disreputable builders in the area and they didn't want to be another victim. They checked around with the Better Business Bureau, and they checked online for reviews, and they talked to friends, and they called out three different pool builders to interview to select one for their project.

Well, they finally chose Brand X Pools. It was owned and operated by Frank xxx. Frank had been building pools for over fifteen years and he seemed to have a good reputation in the area. They talked to three or four of his previous customers and they went out and actually saw some of his projects. They liked what they saw. They could tell that Frank had experience and was building pools that looked really beautiful. Frank seemed to be very conscientious and appeared to be very quality oriented, so they hired Frank to develop a set of plans and an estimate for their project.

The Dream (Nightmare) Begins

About two weeks went by. Frank came back with a beautiful drawing and a detailed list of cost estimates. Everything seemed to be in order so they entered into a contract and construction was scheduled. Finally, the big day arrived and construction had begun. However, they were disappointed right from the start. It seems that the bobcat that's coming into the yard to dig the swimming pool had to come over their existing sod lawn in the front of the house and it tore it up. It left big ruts in the lawn from the tires. Ryan and Sheryl weren't prepared for this and they talked to Frank immediately. Frank said, "This is very common. You know, we have to get the tractor in and out of that backyard to excavate the pool. It's just sod lawn and you can have it replaced after we're done. You can find a landscaper to replace it."

This was a big surprise for Ryan and Sheryl. They didn't expect this. Nobody told them that there was going to be damage to the lawn. From that point on, they had several surprises throughout the construction process. They weren't prepared for subcontractors showing up unannounced and walking in and out of the backyard leaving the gate open and their little dog would escape and run down the street.

Also, many times, subcontractors were working, but Frank wasn't there to supervise them. The subs would knock on their door and ask the homeowners for advice on how to have certain things done. The homeowners had to get on the phone and call Frank and tell him that the sub needs help. They told Frank, "We don't know what to tell the subcontractors. This is something you should have handled already." They were a little surprised that there wasn't hundred percent supervision by Frank when the subs were there. They just assumed if a subcontractor was working that Frank would be there to supervise them.

Lack of Communication

Several more problems seem to crop up as the construction went along. The location of the pool equipment seemed to be blocking a window of the house. They didn't catch that when they're looking at the plain view of the project. Since they are not familiar with blueprints, it should have been pointed out to them that the top of the filter tank is going to be seen through your family room window. Had they known this, they would have chosen a different location for the pool equipment.

When it came time for the concrete work to be done around the pool, the subcontractors showed up with a different color of cool deck than what they had selected. It wasn't the right color. When Frank came out, he told them, "This is the right color. You chose the color off of a brochure and the color on the brochure is always a little different than the actual color we put on the deck." Well, this upset Sheryl quite a bit because this should have been told to them upfront and a real sample given to them prior to making a selection.

Finally, their dream pool was finished and Ryan and Sheryl were somewhat pleased with the final project. However, due to all the problems that surfaced during the construction, they had a bad taste in their mouth for Frank and Brand X Pools. They weren't quite sure they made the right choice at this point. The aggravation factor was just too high. They weren't prepared for a lot of the things that came up during the construction. They felt they could have been prepared a lot better.

Same Old Story

I've been in the swimming pool construction business for over thirty-eight years and I've seen this story of Ryan and Sheryl happen way too many times. The pool builder in this scenario was an honest man. However, he wasn't organized and he didn't have any systems in place to ensure that the construction would go much smoother than it did and he didn't adequately prepare his customers for the construction process.

There's a lot of construction workers, be they roofers, electricians, plumbers, landscapers, or what have you, that know their craft well. They're honest people, but they just focus on getting out there and getting the project done and moving on to the next project. Too often, contractors are not in control of their business. In Frank's case, when things seemed to go wrong as they usually do in major construction projects, he didn't have a plan for handling the problems prior to them arising. He didn't address them with the homeowner and warn them of possible scenarios that could take place.

His failure to communicate with Ryan and Sheryl left them unprepared. Had Frank prepared them prior to the start of the job, their expectations would have been more in line with reality. Had Frank had a pre-construction meeting with the clients and gone over all the negative things that possibly could happen in the next few weeks, Ryan and Sheryl would have been prepared, and it wouldn't have seemed like such a big surprise to them.

I see this happen a lot with contractors. The owner of the construction company knows his craft very well and He might build an excellent product, but he doesn't realize that his business involves a lot of more than just building a product. You have clients, subcontractors and employees to work with, and you better have systems in place to facilitate the entire operation. Without systems you will not be in control. You won't run the company; the company will run you.

Pros Have Systems

Having a lack of systems in place is definitely the biggest and most common mistake Contractors make. Without these systems in place, chaos, costly mistakes and unhappy customers will be commonplace. Professional Contractors have systems for their entire business operation. You should have well defined systems for:

- Lead Generation
- Answering the phone
- Qualifying Customers
- Appointment Setting
- Sales Presentations
- Lead Follow up
- Getting Referrals
- Hiring/Terminations
- Subcontractor Agreements
- Construction Supervision
- Warranty Fulfillment
- Handling Complaints
- Systems and Practices

No doubt, within your organization, you have a sales force. The sales force might be made up of one salesman, or it might be made up of twenty or more. What methods are they using and what kind of presentations are they giving? Are they in fact all giving a different presentation? I propose that there cannot be twenty different ways to most successfully and effectively sell your product. I advise that you discover what is the most effective sales presentation, then develop it, improve on it, and give it to each salesperson, so that when they go out to sell, everyone is on the same page and using the best sales presentation.

Most Salespeople Wing It

When you observe most sales organizations, you'll see people functioning like they did in the wild, wild West with everyone making up his or her own stuff. This is absolutely crazy! Let's first figure out the best way to do this consistently and successfully, and then do it throughout the organization! Consider this: sports teams are run better than most businesses, not only at the college level but also at the pro level. In the NFL, who is the guy with a clip board walking up and down the sideline talking to the players? It's the Head Coach. What is on his clip board? It's the playbook. What is a playbook? Well, it is the play sheet for a particular game against a particular competitor. The play sheet lists the plays designed to be the most effective for their team to enable them to win the game with the resources that they came to play with.

On each sideline, they each have a playbook, and they have practiced, and they have prepared, and they are ready to play. Let me ask you an important question: Where's the playbook of your sales people? Are they going into the field, and have they analyzed their competition? Have they analyzed their prospects? Have they analyzed how their product and service fits up well with that particular customer?" Are they going out into the field like most salespeople and just winging it? How many coaches at the pro level would send their players out on game day without a game plan? How many NFL coaches would send their players out on the field without practicing? How many coaches at the college level? High school coaches of sports teams are preparing their teams better than most businesses. My experience in business is this, that most businesses give a three-part training program to their new salespeople.

Three Part Training

"Here's your cards. Here's your territory. Good luck, baby, and go for it." Then three months later, the management of the company is looking at the sales results, and they're looking at it salesperson by salesperson and they go, "Guys, I thought Bob was going to be a lot better, but his results are not very good. He's just not really that good."

It's not that the person isn't any good. It's that the coach isn't good. What are we doing on the sales management side? What are we doing in terms of preparing our people to play? To play to win? Systems and processes are the keys to running any business.

I loved reading Jim Collins' book, Great By Choice, and if you haven't read it, I'd highly recommend it. In that book, Jim Collins presents the results of a study he conducted of companies that year after year produced increases in sales and profits. He looked at those companies and asked, "What do these highly successful companies have in common?" He discovered that each company was consistent in application of the basics. The systems and processes that they had developed and proven to be effective in the field were run consistently year in and year out throughout the all these companies. It more than apparent that the key to an effective sales force is their adherence to tried and true systems and processes.

Get Back to Mastering the Basics

In Great By Choice, Jim Collins tells the story of American basketball player and coach John Wooden

(1910-2010). Wooden won championships as a player, and, as head coach of the UCLA Bruins, he set a record winning seven NCAA national champions in a row!

When Wooden was head coach at UCLA, his first day of practice was always the same every year.

> *"Gentlemen, take off your shoes and your socks, Today, we're going to show you how to properly put on your socks and lace up your shoes. At UCLA, we never want to find ourselves in a situation where a player of ours can't give us his absolute best, because he's got a blister, because he didn't know how to properly put on his socks. At UCLA Basketball, we never want to have a situation where we have a turnover at a critical juncture in a game, because one of our players tripped over an untied shoelace. Now at UCLA, we will have an understanding of the fundamentals. We will focus on the basics. We will practice those basics and those fundamentals. We will do it with systems and processes, and if we practice the fundamentals and the basics, day in and day out, that scoreboard and that standings will take care of themselves."*

What we want to do is be laser focused on the basics with systems and processes. UCLA won nine out of ten years and were National Champions. That's where I would want to be as a businessperson and that's where I'd want to be as a sales organization. How do we get there? The best way is to model these top sports teams. Develop systems and best practices that are proven to work and train our sales team to use them every time. No more "winging it!"

Developing these systems is going to take a lot of preparation and forethought, but it will make the difference between having an organization that runs on "Automatic" or having one that creates havoc, unhappy customers, and disgruntled employees. And take note:

THESE SYSTEMS WILL NEED TO BE IN WRITING, PLACED IN A BINDER, AND UPDATED AS NEEDED!

Rich Contractors ... have well thought out systems in place.

Poor Contractors ... have no systems and no happy customers.

7

Sub-Contractors

Round up the usual suspects
Captain Renault in Casablanca (1942)

Green Side Up

A general contractor was speaking with a woman about a painting job. In the first room, she said she would like a light blue color. The contractor wrote this down and went to the window, opened it, and yelled out, "Green side up!"

In the second room, she told the contractor she would like the walls painted bright yellow. He wrote this on his pad, walked to the window, opened it, and yelled, "Green side up!" The lady was somewhat curious but she said nothing.

In the third room, she said she wanted a warm beige color. The contractor wrote this down, walked to the window, opened it and yelled, "Green side up!"

The lady then asked him, "Why do you keep yelling 'green side up'?"

"I'm sorry," came the reply. "But I have a crew of sub-contractors laying sod across the street."

Being a contractor would be a fabulous profession if it weren't for two things: unreasonable clients and subcontractors. Unreasonable clients can make your life miserable all through the construction process, and even after you're done. However, a bad subcontractor not only makes your life miserable, but gets you into plenty of hot water, causes lawsuits, and loss of profits.

No Jerks Accepted or Wanted!

Smart contractors have a system in place whereby they weed out potential problem clients and selecting only the best subcontractors. Weeding out problem clients is something that sometimes is hard to do. As a business man, you want all the business you can possibly get; however, you should realize that bad business is bad! You should realize there are certain clients that you do not want to do business with, and you need to turn down business from time to time. You need to learn how to say "no" to certain clients that you realize are going to be a huge problem for you.

Likewise, in selecting subcontractors, you need to select subcontractors that aren't going to be a problem for you as well. In selecting subcontractors, you need to set up a qualification list that will determine whether or not a subcontractor should be hired. This is what I feel consists of six major topics.

Number one: You need to check out the subcontractor's experience. Make sure they have the right experience for the work that you are hiring them to do. Also, you want to make sure that they can handle the size of projects that you typically do. If they are, let's say, a small tile company and they only have one crew, but you, for instance, are doing 80 projects a year and you need tile people to work on 80 projects and they have one crew, you're going to need additional tile subcontractors. Make sure that they are the size of company that can handle your projects. Look for experience. How many years have they been in business doing the type of work that you want them to do for you?

Are They Good Businessmen?

Two: You need to make sure that they have an accountability system in place for their company. In other words, do they have proper supervision of the workers once they're out into the field? Find out who runs their business and who manages the workers actually on the job site. Who are their foremen that are going to be supervising the trade people? You want to make sure that these foremen are the type of people that you can work with.

Three: You need to check out the business management practices of the subcontractor that you're planning on hiring. Is it a well-run business? Are they the type of company that pays their bills? Do they have a good credit rating? Have you checked out other contractors that they're doing business with and find out if they are good business people?

More Than One Law Suit? Don't Walk, Run Away!

Have they been sued in the past? How many lawsuits have they encountered in the past? You could check these out with the local court house filings to see if their company has been sued in the past. I would check also on their reputation. You could do a Google search and uncover information on these particular subcontractors to find out about their credibility. Although the internet will give you some useful information about their reputation, you also have to ask around and get references from these subcontractors, material suppliers. Maybe even their own bank where they do banking.

No insurance Policy? Don't Hire Them!

Lastly, I would check to make sure that each subcontractor that you're going to hire has proper insurance and it's up-to-date. Also, has proper licensing. I have found that some subcontractors who have tried to get me to hire them actually lied about their insurance and their licensing. They would tell you they have insurance. They tell you that they have license, but when you ask them to produce the proof, they can't come up with it. They were hoping you wouldn't ask for the proof, so you must be diligent in finding out if they are license with the state, and do they have up-to-date contractor's insurance.

Also make sure you have each sub-contractor contact their insurance Agent and have your company listed as CO Insured on their policy. This gives you added protection in case they screw up on one of your projects.

When dealing with subcontractors, meet with the owner of the subcontracting firm. Determine whether or not he or she's the type of person that you could actually do business with. Last thing in the world you want to do is hire a subcontractor, and the owner of the subcontracting company is a complete jerk. Make sure your personality is compatible with their personality. Life is too short and you don't need the aggravation.

Have a Written Sub-Contractor Agreement in Place

Lastly, when selecting subcontractors and hiring the subs, you must set up a standard by which they will operate. In other words, you have to agree upon what is expected of the subcontractor, what level of quality are you demanding of them, and what defines quality. I would suggest that you create a formal written agreement and have your subcontractors sign their acceptance that each job that they will do for you as a subcontractor will meet the defined quality criteria, or they will redo the job at no cost to you. This is quality assurance put in writing. After all, the work that these subcontractors are doing is a direct reflection on you and your company. If they do shoddy work, you are going to be seen as a shoddy contractor. The last thing you want to do is hire subcontractors who do subpar work, don't stand behind their work, and create unhappy clients for you. I would suggest it would be a good business practice to have your attorney draw up a subcontractor agreement form and have each subcontractor sign and keep it on file. It might cost four or five hundred dollars to have an agreement form drawn up but it could save you thousands of dollars down the road.

Contractor's Terms

These terms are curtesy of Topfloorstore at http://www.topfloorstore.com.

- **Contractor:** A gambler who never gets to

shuffle, cut or deal.
- **Bid Opening:** A poker game in which the losing hand wins.
- **Low Bidder:** A contractor who is wondering what he/she left out.
- **Engineer's Estimate:** The cost of construction in Heaven.
- **Completion Date:** The point at which liquidated damages begin.
- **Liquidated Damages:** A penalty for failing to achieve the impossible.

Rich Contractors ... hire slow and fire fast, and say no to bad prospects.

Poor Contractors ... hire whoever is available and accept all jobs.

8

There is a Gold Mine in Your Message

Show Me the Money
Jerry Maguire in Jerry Maguire (1996)

There is enough money in your industry and in your market for you to double or triple your sales and revenue in the next year alone. The money in the sales are just sitting right now and waiting for you to come and get them. The problem, the reason why you're not making those sales right now, is because you're doing your marketing and advertising all wrong, and I'm going to prove it to you.

After years of research and study of countless Marketing systems, books, and seminars I happened to come into contact with a very unique individual by the name of Diego Rodrigues. He is the president and founder of Power Marketing Consultants. His organization helps businesses develop and implement a special marketing and sales system that virtually guarantees that their clients will become the number one business in their industry. I was so impressed with this system that I joined the organization as an outside Consultant. I'm going to briefly share with you the highlights of this system. It is a complete marketing system that when executed properly will cause your prospects and customers to realize that you're the only company in your industry they should be doing business with. In fact, I will show you exactly how you can make the advantages of doing business with your company so obvious to your prospects and customers that they quickly and easily draw this conclusion: "I have to be completely insane to work with anyone else but you, no matter the price."

Power Marketing System

The system I'm going to share with you is called the Power Marketing Program and it is unique in our industry because of its comprehensive nature. It's not about running ads or using new technological techniques. In fact, I'm quite certain you've never heard anything like this before. No. You're going to find that the Power Marketing Program covers basically everything that is necessary to ensure that your company becomes number one in your industry. When I say number one, I mean number one.

The purpose of this marketing system is not just to help you acquire a few new customers. If your goal is to learn a tip or two about some simple new little marketing gimmick or a cool direct mail idea or a new Internet marketing trick or a way you get found online or a new graphic or design idea or anything like that, then this is not the program for you. Sure, I'll cover some of that stuff briefly since the program is comprehensive, but that's not we're going to learn here.

With this program, you're going to learn everything you need to know so that you can rise to a place of total dominance. You get that? We're not going to aim at increasing revenue a little here and a little there. We're talking total dominance. I want to show you how you can become the 900-pound gorilla in your industry and in your market and receive all the benefits that come with being number one.

Now before we can really get started explaining to you the details of the 5 steps in the Power Marketing Program, I need to share with you the 2 most common marketing mistakes that nearly all business owners make.

If you've done any advertising or marketing for your business ever at all, I can virtually guarantee you that you've been making at least one of the following 2 common marketing mistakes, and it doesn't matter if you've been doing business for 5, 10, 20, 30 years or more and have been getting what most people would consider pretty good results. I'm here to tell you that these 2 mistakes have cost you a lot of money and lost opportunity and lost business.

I'm not just blowing a bunch of smoke here to catch your attention. In fact, I want you to get some of your marketing material right now. Be it a brochure, a radio script, a TV ad, a newspaper or magazine ad, your website, whatever it is, get access to it right now, and then evaluate it for yourself as I describe these 2 mistakes. I want you to objectively judge your own marketing and advertising and make a determination for yourself whether or not what I'm saying has value, so let's begin.

Two Biggest Marketing Mistakes

Mistake number one is using one of the 3 forbidden phrases, so what are the 3 forbidden phrases? Well, they are phrases that use platitudes.

In marketing, platitudes are essentially the kiss of death, so let me give you the definition of a platitude as it pertains to marketing. Platitudes are "words or phrases that are dull, obvious, or predictable that lack power to create interest because they are overused and unoriginal, that are nevertheless still commonly used as though they were unique or distinctive."

Let me give you some examples of platitudes. They are words and phrases like …

Highest Quality
Best Service
Largest Selection
Gets the Job Done Right the First Time
30 Years of Experience
Been in Business Since 1776 B.C.
Honest
Hard Working
You've Tried the Rest, Now Try the Best
Number One
Your Dealer of Choice
State-of-the art

Does it sound familiar? Of course it does. You've heard this kind of garbage for years, but now here's the killer question: Do you have these terms in your marketing? I bet you do. I don't even know you, but if I were a betting man, which I'm not, I would bet the farm on the fact that your advertising and marketing is loaded with platitudes just like these right now. Take a look for yourself.

Now here's the takeaway. These platitudes that fill up your marketing and advertising are killing your profits and eliminating your market opportunities. These platitudes don't distinguish or separate you in the marketplace; they don't quantify or specify anything. They're not believable. They usually are not provable and they cause your prospects to minimize, discount, disbelieve, or ignore you all together. Ultimately your target market ends up believing that you and your business are just like everybody else in your industry. This is why your target market always ends up beating you up on price, regardless of how great you claim your service is or how much better you think you are than your competitors. None of that matters because you've introduced yourself to the marketplace as one more Contractor in a whole city full of Contractors.

Evaluate Your Advertising

And you know if you're perceived as being common, just like everyone else, the only real message you're portraying to your target market is me too. Now think about how unprofitable that is. You see, this is why you're not dominating your market, and this is why your sales and revenues are dependent upon the force of the market and not your ability to win over more and more customers and dominate your sector. Now that's a big difference. Let me break this down further for you by using some objective evaluations so you can determine if you really are using platitudes in your advertising or not.

I want to take you through 3 platitude evaluations that come directly out of Rich Harshaw's book,

Monopolize Your Marketplace. We touched upon this in Chapter 3. I am more than familiar with Rich Harshaw, who is a living marketing genius, and I have trained directly with Diego Rodriquez, President of Power Marketing. Let's review these 3 evaluations which expose what we call the "Three Forbidden Phrases."

Platitude evaluation number one is called "Well, I would hope so." Seriously, that's the name of the first evaluation. When you make a statement like "We do it right the first time", what do you think your customer is thinking? He is thinking "Well I would hope so! A marketing claim like this makes you look ridiculous.

Platitude evaluation number two is, "Who else can say that?" Does your advertising boast about things your company does that all your competitors can also do as well?

Platitude evaluation number three is the scratch out and write in test. Take your brochure or a recent advertisement and scratch out your name and replace it with the name of one of your competitors. Is it still valid? If it is, then your ads stink big time!

Fragmented Marketing

The second most common marketing mistake that businesses make is what we call fragmented or piece-meal marketing. This is absolutely the wrong approach to marketing, yet it is the most common approach in business today. Everybody is doing it, including you and your competitors. The good news or bad news if you're slow, is that the first one to fix this problem basically wins. Seriously.

Fragmented Marketing Has No Impact

Now let me explain fragmented marketing, which is the wrong way to do it in contrast to what we call systematized marketing, which is the right way to do it. Fragmented marketing means that there's no cohesive message or comprehensive system handling your marketing for you. Instead when you buy marketing and advertising, it is developed by the company creating the ad, right? Think back to the last advertisement or marketing piece that you created for your company. What was it? A brochure, a website, a printed ad, a radio spot? Now let me ask you a question: Who created the final product for you? They did, didn't they? The radio station created your radio spot, the magazine created your magazine ad, the design company created your brochure, the web design company created the website, and the video production company developed the content for your video. Right?

Think about how fragmented that makes your marketing efforts. All of those different companies have different ideas about what your marketing message should be based on their limited experience.

Inevitably, they all use platitudes and then they try to throw in their own dose of creativity. Think about how wrong this is. You need to develop and own your own message. You shouldn't leave it to others, and you certainly shouldn't leave it to multiple teams of others who don't really have your best interest in mind, nor do they care about your position in the marketplace.

This is why you need a marketing system in place. The system dictates the content of the advertisements and it dictates the sequence that your prospects go through and the message that your prospects hear as they are ultimately led to your door. A systematized marketing program would actually facilitate the decision-making process. In other words, it would define what criteria your prospect should look for in a company, product, or service, and in doing so, it would lead them to buy from you and not your competitor.

Content Is King

Here's another question to illustrate this problem. Take a look at your last advertisement. I know, it's filled with platitudes, but here's the question: How much money did you pay to have the content of that advertisement strategically created and formulated to ensure maximum results? I'm not talking about the design. I'm talking about the content, the message, what you actually said in the advertisement. Not what it looks like. See that's what I thought: you paid nothing right? 99.9% of the time you only pay to have the advertisement produced or designed, or you paid for the spots or airtime. The content was usually just thrown together by the designer, the production team, or the salesperson. Think about it, the most important part of your marketing material, that is the content and message was put together for free by people who usually have no idea how to create good messaging anyway.

Have you ever heard the saying, "You get what you pay for?" Well, I hate to tell you this, but if you've never paid anybody to create the actual message or content for your advertising campaigns, then you got what you paid for.

Here's the point. When you think of marketing, you need to start thinking about your message, you need to think about what you're going to say, and how you're going to say it. When you think of marketing, don't think of mediums anymore, think of messaging. Only once you have the right message, should you then start considering which mediums to run your marketing in.

You see, this is the difference between a marketing system and typical fragmented marketing. A marketing system considers first the message, then it develops the message and installs the message in a comprehensive marketing system, which facilitates the prospects' decision-making process. Finally, it chooses the best mediums to put those messages in to generate leads to pump into the system. Do you see how much more effective that is than typical fragmented marketing?

You might be asking yourself, why are we all using platitude? It seems so obvious that it's the wrong way to do it, but everybody is doing it. Well, I don't want to spend too much time answering that question, because I want to get to the solutions quickly for you, but the answer to this question is actually more important than you realize and understanding the answer to this question is essential in order for you to be able to fix the problem.

The Invisible Gorilla

Have you ever seen the "Invisible Gorilla experiment?" If not, let me explain it to you. The experiment was devised by Dan Simons who received his PhD in experimental psychology from Cornell University. You can find the video on YouTube by typing in Invisible Gorilla into the search field.

Anyhow, in the video, there are 3 students with white shirts and 3 students with black shirts. The white team passes a basketball to one another and the black team does the same, but the catch is they're all moving around and walking in and amongst one another. Your job as the observer is to count how many times the team with the white shirts passes the ball to one another. That's it. The video only lasts about 20 seconds, but here's where it gets funny.

In the middle of the video, a guy wearing a gorilla suit walks right into the video frame, stands right in front of the camera, faces the camera, leans back, pounds his chest, and then walks out of the camera frame. It's hilarious, because he's right there in front of your face pounding his chest, but guess what? Most people watching the video never see the gorilla. I'm serious. I know it's hard to believe, but it's true. Check out the video on YouTube for yourself.

I have showed the video to dozens of people, and

my personal experience has been that well over 80% of people I show it to, never see the gorilla. In fact, I always hope that at least 1 person in the group sees the gorilla, because if not, my audience accuses me of showing 2 different videos. You know why? Because humans simply cannot believe that a full size gorilla could walk right in front of their face, pound his chest, and walk away without them ever noticing, but it's true. It's unbelievably true. You see, it's just part of human nature. The reason why it happens is because the viewer is distracted counting basketball passes. You see, if the viewer was not given the task of counting basketball passes, basically 100% of all people would see the gorilla, but because people are distracted with another task, they completely miss these incredibly obvious things happening right in front of them.

This is the exact same way that street magicians and pickpockets operate. They are called masters of misdirection because they have learned how to focus your attention on something else while they're stealing your wallet, watch, or purse, or producing a card from a card deck to impress you. Think about how that applies to your work. Are you pretty focused on running your business? I bet you are. I bet you're a very effective and focused business person who runs his business pretty efficiently, or at least you're trying, but think about that as it pertains to marketing.

Focus On the Marketing First

If you're distracted by industry news reports, inventory, profit and loss sheets, HR issues, turnover, insurance, sales forecasts, personnel problems, payroll, and the other 273 relevant issues that you need to pay attention to so that you can effectively run your business, it's highly likely that some very obvious and important gorillas are pounding their chest in front of your face and you're missing them all together. In fact, the same goes for other areas of your life with your relationships, your family, your health, your faith, and other important things. You should really consider that.

Anyhow, we're talking about marketing right now and I want to help you understand where this invisible gorilla came from in marketing and advertising. For the sake of this discussion, the invisible gorilla represents the 2 common mistakes we just discussed. That is using platitudes and using fragmented marketing. In order to understand this, we need to take a quick trip down memory lane.

Let's go back to the late 1800s. Back then, advertising in America was done mostly in a local or regional level, and because of that, the advertising was very comparative and the competition was really fierce. Advertisers didn't use lame platitudes. Instead, they were very specific about why you should buy from them and not their competitors. This continued all the way through the middle of the 20th century, but then, the most significant change in the history of advertising came to America around 1945. It was then that television was first introduced commercially to America. By the time the 50s rolled around, the typical American family had 1 television set, but it only received 3 channels.

Television Changed Advertising Dramatically

Here's the thing. People were enamored with this new device and they basically sat around every night watching it. It was a powerful opportunity. Some of the biggest companies in the country saw the opportunity and jumped on it. They realized that they could reach pretty much everybody in the whole country using the TV and they could do it for pretty cheap. I mean, they could buy a TV commercial and almost reach everybody in the entire country for around $4000 a minute. I mean it was a deal of the century, even in 1950s money.

Once this began to catch on, the price for commercials skyrocketed. It's simple supply and demand. Local and regional advertisers started disappearing because they couldn't afford the higher rates, so the ads were all dominated by larger national companies. Since these large advertisers were already large and had national distribution, the results from these TV commercials were huge, so they happily paid the money.

As the advertising prices rose, the length of the average commercial shrank down and down until it finally got to an average of 30 seconds. You may or not remember, but they used to be about 2 minutes long, but here's why this is all important to you. With only 30 seconds available, advertisers lost the opportunity to really educate their prospects. There was no time available, so instead they started using slogans. They did not explain why they were better, what their unique selling proposition was, or what gave them the competitive edge. Instead, it was all slogans and platitudes simply because of lack of time.

Large advertisers discovered that, because there were relatively few competitors competing on the national stage, they could just spend money and win automatically. They didn't have to be better, they didn't have to be unique, they didn't have to offer better service or quality. They could simply pony up the big bucks on TV commercials and then laugh all the way to the bank. If there were a few competitors, that was fine because there was enough business to split 2 or 3 ways. This is why we ended up with 2 or 3 major players in most national industries. We have Ford, GM, and Chrysler. There's Pepsi and Coke, etc.

Ultimately, what happened is that advertisements lost their sales and marketing function and instead became all about creativity and design: "Hey, let's create something funny, cute, entertaining, and then imprint it on everybody's brains by playing it a billion times on TV and we'll win." "Melts in your mouth, not in your hand. Like a good neighbor, State Farm is there. Don't leave home without it. Fly the friendly skies. Aren't you glad you use Dial?" How about this one: Don't squeeze the ... that's right, "Don't squeeze the Charmin." How'd you know that? That commercial hasn't run for several decades.

Creativity Does Not Sell

Anyhow, creativity, slogans, and platitudes took over and began to fill every advertising medium: radio, newspaper, magazines, billboards, yellow pages, you name it. In fact, they even teach this kind of junk in business colleges and universities, because they think that this is the way to do it. Hey, after all, all of these companies have made their millions doing marketing this way, so it must be right. Right? Yeah, not quite. Not even close.

Here's the big problem. Nearly everybody today involved in advertising and marketing, including marketing graduates, marketing directors, business owners, and advertising salespeople all grew up in an era of creativity, slogans, and platitudes. What do they do when it's time to create their own marketing and advertising? Well, they call upon their memory banks and pull up all the advertising and marketing that they've ever seen in their life and use it as a model to create their own advertising and marketing, and the result is that they come up with a bunch of platitudes and lame slogans.

It's the invisible gorilla in the advertising industry. Everybody is doing it the wrong way even in your industry, but here's the beautiful part about it all. The first one to fix this problem wins.

If you will take a step back and look at the marketplace again, you'll see there's a big gorilla pounding its chest at you, and, if you'll just follow the system at Power Marketing, you can take your company on the path towards total dominance.

Rich Contractors ... use Strategic Messaging in their marketplaces.

Poor Contractors ... use old, outdated marketing methods.

9

The Power Marketing Program

Crush the Competition
Vince Lombardi (1913-1970)

In the last chapter we identified some of the problems with existing advertising in marketing; let's talk about the solution.

The solution to these marketing in advertising problems is the Power Marketing Program. The Power Marketing Program isn't entirely original. In short, we've combined some of the best elements of multiple well known marketing systems and experts including: J. Abraham, Michael Gerber from The E-Myth, Rich Harshaw, Dan Kennedy, Steve Jobs, Claude Hopkins, and others to create one complete and cohesive marketing system that gives your business the leverage to dominate your market. So, it is quite possible that a few elements we'll discuss here and there may sound similar to things you learned before, but I'm confident that you have not heard anything like what I'm about to share with you. Where we've put it all together and developed a comprehensive system that gives you the leverage you need to rise to total dominance.

Give Them What They Want

One of the most important components to a powerful marketing program is business innovation. Believe it or not, your very first marketing opportunity comes down to what you offer the market as a business. In other words, what is it about your company that is unique and distinctive that gives your customers a reason to buy from you instead of any one of your competitors. Some people call this a unique selling proposition or a USP.

The idea here is that you need something that is legitimately unique about your business that makes people feel like they should buy from you. Something that lets people know that you're not just a commodity and that you're not just like everybody else. However, we call this a business innovation because the best way to come up with a USP or a unique selling proposition is to innovate your business, service, or product and to give the marketplace exactly what they want. Plus, once you come up with something truly innovative, it's incredibly simple to write headlines for that innovation.

Let me give you a few examples, let's say you innovated the car and you created a car that runs on water instead of gas or electricity. Pretty innovative right?

So what would you say in the end? What would be your headline? How about "efficient and environmentally friendly". No, of course not. You see how utterly ridiculous those platitudes sound? But that's basically the equivalent of what most companies today are doing. Building great businesses with incredible products and services and then telling the marketplace that they are "efficient and environmentally friendly". In other words, platitudes. Look, writing a headline for innovative products and services is easy. You simply make the innovation a big fat headline., For example, in the case of a car that runs on water, you use a headline that says "This car runs on water" exclamation point. I'd probably add the sub headline that says "seriously". So, the headline and sub headline will be huge and would say this, "This car runs on water, seriously". Of course, there would be a picture of the car there. But you see how that passes the three platitude evaluations? That's not something that you would expect, so it passes the "well, I would hope so" test.

Certainly, no one else can say it and it definitely passes the cross out writing test. I mean, we're talking about a car that runs on water for crying out loud. It's more than just innovative, it's enough to change the world. Now, that's an oversimplified example using an extremely innovative concept, but let's break it down in your world. To come up with an innovation, you simply have to ask yourself one simple question. "What does my marketplace want or need that nobody is offering them?" It's that simple but here's the catch. You must answer the question without regards to your ability to fulfill that need. Just ask the question and answer it. Don't tell yourself, "But I can't do that because it's too expensive" or "I don't have the man power or the experience" or whatever. Just answer the question. Once you have the answer figure out how to give it to your customers. You might not be able to give them 100% of what they want, but even if you give them 50% it's better than anybody else and it makes you innovative.

Let me give you a few examples of contractors since competition on local level with contractors is pretty fierce. One of Power Marketing's clients is a heating and air conditioning contractor. We determined that one of the biggest problems with his industry is that people feel uncomfortable with most service technicians who come into their home to fix their furnace or air conditioning system. So what's the answer to this problem? Well, most contractors say that their technicians are all background checked and drug tested and that they wouldn't send anybody to your house that they wouldn't send to theirs or whatever. Take a look in your area and you'll find these kinds of claims, but here's the problem. Those are all platitudes. I mean, who else can say that? How about everybody? They all say that their technicians are background checked and drug tested and guess what. Did you know that over 80% of heating and air technicians learn their trade in prison because it's the second most commonly taught trade in federal prisons, right behind plumbing?

That means that when a repair technician is at your house with your wife and kids, there's an over 80% likelihood that he's an ex con. How comfortable does that make you feel? So we innovated the business and produced a code of ethics and competency guide for heating and air conditioning companies. This is a one page document that lists 20 year requirements for service technicians that include the obvious things like background checks and drug tests and additional items are on competency standards, personal and ethical requirements, and dress code and appearance. It even guarantees that the customer will receive $100 cash on the spot if the technician uses profanity while on the job. So now we can simply advertise that our company is the only company in the state that requires all of it's service technicians to be certified in the code of ethics and competency guide for heating and air conditioning companies. Who else can say that? Nobody. Does it pass the "well, I would hope so" test? Yes. Does it pass the "cross out write in" test? Yes.

Hit The Hot Buttons

We did the same thing with one of my clients here in Brentwood who's a plumber. The same problems and fears in your industry is also in the plumbing industry. In fact, the stigma for plumbers is even worse because over 90% of plumbers out there today learned their trade in prison. In this case, my client wasn't willing to be as aggressive as the heating and air company, but we ended up creating something similar. In this case, it's called the customer's bill of rights for the plumbing industry. We created a one-page document that list a whole bunch of guarantees and rights that customers receive when doing business with this plumber. We then pitch that Super Router Plumbing is proud to abide by the Customer's Bill of Rights for the Plumbing Industry which protects our customers from any negative experience they might otherwise have from a plumbing company.

Who else can say that? Nobody. Does it hit on a major hot button for the marketplace about getting ripped off by a plumber? Yes. Is there anybody else in the market place who's doing anything like it? No. Does it increase the marketplace awareness that they can have a very negative experience with a plumber repair while simultaneously increasing their confidence that super router plumbing has effectively solved this problem and protects them from such negative experiences? Yes. And that's the key. It increases their confidence.

See. That's what people really want. They just want the unshakable confidence that your company, product, or service is the very best in terms of value. They don't want to feel like they got ripped off or could have gotten a better deal. This brings us to this incredibly important point. Remember what I'm about to say right now and don't forget it. Here it is. The amount of money somebody is willing to give you is directly proportional to their confidence in your ability to provide them with the goods and services that they want or need. Period. Let me say that again for sake of emphasis. The amount of money somebody is willing to give you is directly proportional to their confidence in your ability to provide them with the goods and services that they want or need.

People Buy Confidence

Now, you've heard before that the way to increase profits is to increase the value or perceived value that you offer to your customers, but I'm here to tell you that this type of thinking is antiquated, outmoded, and just flat out wrong, and by wrong I mean that it is missing a critical element. The missing element is confidence. This is actually what people buy, not value. See, value is a result or consequence of confidence. In other words, the more confidence I have in your ability to provide me with the goods and service that I want or need, then the more value you have in my eyes and the more money I'll be willing to give you. Too many people think that the way to increase prices and perceived value is to add additional products and services or to reduce prices, but this is the wrong methodology. Invest your time, energy, and resources into increasing people's confidence in your product, services, and company; and your price points and profits will increase. The key is confidence.

Let me give you some examples. Would you buy a Big-Mac at McDonald's for $20? No. Why not? Because you know it's not worth $20. But what if McDonald's added value to the Big-Mac by adding a large fry and a coke for free. Now would you buy the Big-Mac for $20? Of course not, but what if they added more value by giving you a free happy meal toy? Still the answer is no. Why? Because you know that no matter what additional free stuff they add, it's still not worth $20. What? Would you buy a filet-mignon steak from a major steak house like Donovan's or Ruth's Chris, or Morton's for $20? Of course you would! What a deal! But why the difference? The Big-Mac is made out of 100% pure beef, right? So is the filet-mignon. So why are you willing to buy one and not the other? Because you're confident that one of them is worth more than $20 and the other is not. It's that simple. Winning in the game of business and sales is an issue of confidence. Perception and value are both consequences of confidence.

On Your Way to Total Dominance

So, invest in building your market's confidence in your company, your products, and your services and you'll be on your way to total dominance. So obviously in terms of innovation, there's a big difference in a car that runs on water and the code of ethics and competency guide for heating and air companies or the Customer's Bill Of Rights For The Plumbing Industry, but that's the point. I want you to see and realize that while they are very different in terms of value, they are exactly the same in terms of principle. The principle here is to provide something innovative to the marketplace that they actually want or need. Now it is possible that you already have something innovative in your business. If that's the case, then it's incredibly important that you present this innovation as something unique to the market place. You should name it and trademark it and make it exclusive to your company. Let me give you one more quick example.

One of Power Marketing's clients is the oldest emergency food supply company in the country. They have provided nitrogen packed and sealed food for over 40 years. Now normally the "been in business for 40 years" statement is a major platitude and is basically meaningless, but in their case it actually matters and here's why. Most emergency food supply companies are advertising that their food lasts 10, 15, or 20 years, but the companies themselves haven't even been in business for that long, so how do they know? They don't. Our client has been in business for over 40 years and they've actually tested their food products after 20, 25, and 30 years, and it's still good. I know because we've tasted some of their 30-year-old food myself after opening up one of their sealed containers in their office and having a sample. So, that is definitely a unique selling proposition that we brought to light. However, through the course of our discovery meeting, we found that one of the most pressing problems that people have with the emergency food is that they don't know how much to get or how much they'll need or how to store it or how to prepare it or anything like that.

Most of those things could be answered on their website or other marketing material, but people wanted confidence that they're getting the right stuff. After all, if there's an emergency like a flood, a storm, a tornado, a hurricane, an earthquake, or whatever and I need to get into my emergency food supply, I want to make sure that I have everything I need to eat and feed my family, and I want to make sure that I have enough. Now most companies in the industry have tried to offload this task to online calculators which are insufficient.

Now in our client's case, they actually have trained their customer service staff on the phone to be able to give custom consultations to every customer who calls in. They have a series of questions that they ask them about their wants and needs. They find out the size of their family, their eating preferences, and where they live so they can help them determine future risks. For example, if they live on a fault line or on the coast of hurricane alley, they have higher risks that someone living in a relatively safe valley in the mid-west.

They then custom develop a package for each customer based on this information and their needs. What other companies were doing this? None. How many customers wanted this? Most everyone.

But most customers aren't even aware of these issues and don't even know that they should be asking for it, and of course, our client was using the same old platitudes as everybody else in the industry, just talking about how they need to buy emergency food so they can be prepared and weather the storm or how they were the leader in emergency food supplies or how they were recommended by some radio host.

We asked the client if he had been advertising these custom consultations that they give their customers. He said no. In fact, he didn't even consider them to be custom consultations. It was just a regular service they gave to each one of their clients, after all, that's what people needed, right? Yes. He was right about their needs, but he didn't realize how unique and innovative he was in this case and this highlights another major problem. Our client was so distracted by his business operations that he couldn't see the forest for the trees.

Innovate Your Marketing

It was like an invisible gorilla. He had a great service and innovation that he didn't even realize was great because he did it every day, but nobody else was doing it and everybody needed it. So, we didn't have to innovate his company. We simply innovated the way he marketed his features to the marketplace. First, we changed the names of their customer service representatives. They became emergency food preparedness counselors or EFP counselors for short.

Then, we created videos and other marketing collateral touting the fact that my client always prepared foods, is the only company in the industry with these EFP counselors.

Here's the actual line from their newly updated marketing material: "Always prepared foods has unmatched expertise and experience since we have been in continuous operations longer than any company in the industry. We have taken this expertise and trained all of our emergency preparedness counselors to consult and advise each one of our customers. We understand that people often don't know what they need in order to be prepared. Don't worry. Just give us a call and one of our trained EFP counselors will give you professional advice so you can have peace of mind."

You Set the Standard

Are you starting to see how this works? We're

giving the marketplace the criteria by which they should judge companies, products, and services, and then we make sure that we know that we're the only ones who fit that criteria. It's powerful marketing. So, finally, let me give you a tool that you can use to create your own business innovations.

We actually have 12 innovation formulas that we use that allow us to easily and scientifically find needs and desires in any industry or marketplace and then create unique innovations to fill those needs and desires that can easily be implemented by our clients. Some are more advanced than others but in every case a true and exclusive business innovation is developed so that our clients distinguish themselves in the marketplace.

I present only one of these 12 innovation formulas below. To get the other eleven, just email me at mikelogan63@gmail.com.

Find Their Biggest Problem and Fix It!

This one is called the ultimate solution. It's remarkably simple yet powerful. Here's all you need to do. Write down on a piece of paper a negative situation that your customers could or would have when doing business with someone in your industry. Let's say you're a dentist. Write down the negative experiences that people have with dentists. Now there are a lot of them. They could be problems relating to fear, or pain, or costs, or problems with insurance payments, or the problem's just waiting too long, or whatever. Just write down the potential negative experiences.

Then ask yourself this killer question. "If your customers had the power to change anything in your business to solve this problem, what would they do to alleviate the problem?" In other words, what would the ultimate business do to ensure that this problem never existed? What is the ultimate solution? Brainstorm answers to this question with everybody. Just let it rip. Write everything down on paper. Do not exclude any ideas just because they're not practical. In fact, if at least 50% of your ideas are not impractical, then you'll never innovate anything significant.

I'll use a ridiculously simple example so you can understand the methodology here. Though in the real world, I expect you to come up with some much better innovations than this example. So let's innovate the dentist really quick in regards to the waiting experience. The problem here is that people have an appointment and they show up on time but then they have to wait 15 to 20 minutes before they are seen. So here are some innovations. How about a guarantee that if you're not seen within five minutes of scheduled appointment that you get a free teeth cleaning? How about getting a free neck massage while you wait for your appointment?

Hey, if my dentist has someone giving me a neck massage while I was waiting for my appointment, I would actually look forward to every appointment and get there early. I'd also brag about my cool dentist to everybody I know. How about this. 50 different magazines in the waiting area in all categories with current issues. How about wireless internet connections for your laptop? Computer stations with internet. How about instead of a waiting room, have a home theater set up playing Imax documentaries all day or at least have leather recliners or snacks and drinks for free or video games and video simulators. How about a live band? Okay, well maybe that's too much, but hey, maybe it's not. Again, if at least half of your ideas aren't crazy or impractical, you'll never come up with anything good, so just let it rip.

Remember your objective is to ensure that the business innovations you come up with build your customers confidence in your ability to provide them with the goods and services that they want or need. We'll talk more about confidence in the next chapter. Here's a final point I want to make about innovation. Innovation is not just a business function. It's actually a core part of your marketing program. Simply put, if you want to dominate your sector of the market, you must be innovative. You cannot expect to win the lion's share of the marketplace by being just like everybody else. Furthermore, you can't just be different for the sake of being different. Your innovation must address real and legitimate wants and/or needs of your target market.

Rich Contractors ... are innovative and instill confidence plus value.

Poor Contractors ... try adding value alone

10

Strategic Messaging Formula

I'm the King of the World!
Jack Dawson in Titanic (1997)

Okay, so now that we've identified some of the problems with existing advertising in marketing, let's talk about solutions. I want to show you exactly what your marketing content is supposed to look like. Believe it or not, the process of creating effective strategic marketing programs is actually scientific. You've been taught to believe that marketing is an art, and that you need a team of creative people to invent funny, quirky, entertaining, or any other type of creative content to use in your advertising and marketing. This is simply not the case.

Years ago there was a marketing acronym used called, AIDA. It stood for Attention, Interest, Desire, and Action. In his book, Monopolize your Marketplace, Rich Harshaw updated this formula and called it the "Marketing Equation." Both of these systems worked well for years, and still do.

However, in today's internet age with so much information being disseminated online, and with incredibly software tools available to us, along with our own testing in the Power of Marketing Consultant's Network, we have refined this system even further. We call this scientific method for creating comprehensive marketing systems, "The strategic messaging formula," and we use it exclusively within the Power of Marketing Consultants Network to generate industry leading results for all of our customers no matter their industry.

Ultimately the goal of the strategy messaging formula is to cause your customers and prospects to draw in this important conclusion that you've heard several times already, "I have to be completely insane to work with anyone but you, no matter the price." Don't you want your customers and prospects thinking that way? Of course you do. Let me show you how this works.

Capture Their Attention

The Strategic Messaging Formula, or SMF for short, has five components. Let me introduce them to you really quick.

First, is **CAPTURE**. This means that you must first capture your target markets attention. It's pretty obvious, I know. It's not easy to pull off as people think. Furthermore, it's done wrong more often than it's done right. You'll learn how and why in a minute.

The second component is **CONNECT**. This means that once you've captured your prospects attention, you must connect with them on an emotional level. You have to hold onto their attention by connecting with a hot button that is important or relevant to them. You have to make them feel like important and relevant information is going to be delivered to them. Information that will help them make the best decision possible. In short, you will be helping to facilitate the decision making process.

The third component is **INFORM**. Now that you've connected with your prospect on an emotional level, you must give them enough quality information to make them feel like they can make an informed decision about how to solve their problem, or gain a needed benefit. Again, you do this by giving your prospect enough quality information to address their emotional need. Remember, the component is called, "Inform." You are informing them. This step is ultra-critical, and it turns the sale from an emotional sale, to a logical one.

The fourth component is **INCENTIVIZE**. You in this step you have to give your prospect an incentive to take the next step in the buying process. This is often accomplished by giving your prospect an offer to get a free marketing tool of some sort. A special report, a book, a video, a series of videos, an marketing program, or anything like that.

However, you don't always have to give away a marketing tool. Often you can give them a coupon, an exclusive discount, a special limited opportunity, or any other low risk or high value offer. Whatever it is, just remember that you're incentivizing your prospect. You are simply getting them to take the next step in the buying process.

The fifth and final component is **AUTOMATE**. This simply means that now that your prospects are connected with you and your marketing system, you must create content to automate the follow up process. Companies and individuals are notoriously bad about following up. Fortunately, software's available today to assist in the process. Even then, the software will not give you the best bang for your buck if you don't properly craft your message in follow up sequence. We're going to show you exactly how to accomplish this in the next few tricks.

The acronym for the strategic messaging formula is CCIIA. The easiest way to remember it is to think of the CIA, but with two C's, and two I's. Just like the CIA is the Central Intelligence Agency for the United States, the world's greatest superpower. The strategic messaging formula is the brains and center of your comprehensive marketing system. Capture, connect, inform, incentivize, and automate. It's a proven formula for marketing success. It's a scientific approach to marketing that is based on human nature, and when properly executed, drives your prospects and customers to this conclusion. Go ahead and say it with me, "I'd have to be completely insane to work with anybody else but you, no matter the price."

Systemized Sales Process

Step four in the power of marketing program is to create and implement a systematized sales process as mentioned in chapter 2. This is one of the most overlooked aspects of a complete marketing system.

Those who utilize it will increase sales and maximize efficiencies, while simultaneously driving revenue and lowering cost. Sounds good, right? It almost sounds too good to be true, but it's not. It's just called the guaranteed results that come from hard work done right. A lot of what we do here comes from Michael Gerber's book called, "The Email." If you've never read that book then you need to read it' it's one of the best-selling business books ever written, and it's worth its weight in gold.

No System...No Success

In short Michael Gerber describes the reason why most businesses fail, and that reason is that most small business owners are experts at their trade or craft, but they're not experts at running a business. It's a big difference, and it's the difference that makes the difference. Michael's solution to the problem is to create and implement systems in your business to do the heavy lifting for you, so that your business is a streamlined and nearly automated machine that makes money for you, without your need for constant and perpetual oversight. That's the over simplified explanation of what the book is about, but that's the gist of it.

In our case we've created this step in the Power of Marketing program to ensure the entire sales and marketing process is systematized. We don't want to leave anything to chance, especially considering how much work is involved in creating our marketing programs for our customers.

Here's an important analogy, think about how much effort and infrastructure goes into creating a newspaper. I know, I know, newspapers are dying, and they'll be extinct in a generation, but just ride with me for a moment. In order to produce just one newspaper, the publisher has to employ a small army of people to gather news information, write news articles, edit them, types in the content, lay out the paper, design the ads, sell the ads, and then actually have printing presses and press operators in place to run overnight while we sleep so that the most recent news is available to us the morning. It's an incredible amount of effort and infrastructure, all designed to get you to read the paper.

After all the effort that goes into producing just one paper, the paperboy takes the paper and throws it in the mud. Then what? Will a prospect even read the paper? No, they won't. All of the effort and infrastructure developed by the publisher is ruined in one split second when the paperboy throws it in the mud. What a bummer, eh? The same goes for your business. No matter how much effort you put into creating the most incredible business in your industry, and no matter how well articulated your marketing and advertising is, it can all be ruined in a split second during the sales process. If your sales people don't have a systematized sales process to follow, they could throw your company in the mud at the last minute right before your products or services were properly delivered to your prospect.

A Case Study of Success

The way to overcome this is with a complete systematized sales process. Let me walk you through a case study with a contractor so you can see what this would look like. Like I mentioned earlier, one of my clients is a local contractor who sells heating and air conditioning systems and repair, otherwise known as HVAC or H-V-A-C. That stands for Heating, Ventilation, and Air Conditioning. When my client first came to me he was using all the typical platitudes that every other contractor was using. You know, been in business since 1776BC, Same day service, licensed, bonded, and insured, and all the rest of that junk.

The perception was that he was pretty much like everybody else. However, the reality is that they were unquestionably the most innovative company in the industry. So innovative in fact, that I didn't have to create one new innovation for them. We simply innovated the way we described his unique selling propositions to the marketplace. My client, we'll call him Jim, built his business, Express Heating and Cooling, to be the best in the industry. He didn't need any help there, but Jim's marketing suffered because he wasn't using the power of marketing program.

Let me describe the entire marketing system for you. First of all, we created dozens of headlines with different offers for different mediums. We started with the internet and the Yellow Pages, because HVAC is one of the few industries where prospects still look businesses up in the phone book. On the internet, we built online presence so that our customer was everywhere. He has a custom designed Facebook page, Google Plus page, Twitter Account, and YouTube channel. We post new updates every week on all of his social media accounts, and his YouTube channel has over 20 videos relating to his industry. His videos dominate the search results for any of his relevant search phrases in YouTube, and we've done SEO for his website so his website shows up on page one for his most profitable keywords.

In fact, for his number one most profitable keyword, he was showing up three times on page one of Google. Once under the map section, once under the organic listing, and once as a video. In short, he was dominating. When visitors get to his website they are greeted with a popup video that only plays the very first time you visit, and never again. The video is from the owner himself, who thanks visitors for coming, and then offers them an immediate discount on a repair by filling out the form on the website. In his industry there's also a lot of skepticism, so we developed one of the most advanced testimonial sections on any website ever.

The More Testimonies the Better

When you click on the testimonial page there are three sets of testimonials. The first are actual audio recordings of phone calls from customers who have called in and given testimonials while speaking with customer service representatives. There are dozens of them. Below that there's video testimonials from customers who shared their positive experiences. Then beneath that are well over a 1,000 signed testimonials in PDF format from customers raving about their experience with Express Heating and Cooling. They're all conveniently arranged by zip code, so you can click on your zip code and find testimonials from dozens of your neighbors.

Also, we created another popup video on the testimonial page with the owner Jim describing the testimonial page. He proudly proclaims that on this page, "You'll find more testimonials than you've probably ever seen in your life." You know what? It's true. Have you ever been to a website with over 1,000 testimonials in three formats on one page for a local contractor, or for any industry for that matter? I didn't think so. You see, I'm not playing Patty Cake here folks, we're seeking total dominance in the industry.

In the Yellow Pages we used a double ad with one full page dedicated to service and repairs, and the other full page dedicated to new sales. The service and repair side had a headline that said, "We are the only company in Idaho that offers all of this." We then go onto list eight features that no other company offers.

Some highlight to things like a true money back service guarantee that states if you're simply not satisfied with the service you receive, you get your money back. Nobody offers that. Lots of companies offer satisfaction guarantees, but not money back guarantees. The satisfaction guarantee essentially means nothing because it's so subjective. You're not satisfied, so then what? The same company that made you dissatisfied sends somebody out to do it again? I mean how lame is that?

Strong Guarantees = Client Confidence

In our case if your dissatisfied for any reason, you get your money back. How is that for confidence? Based on that alone which heating and air company would you want to use? The one who proudly proclaims to be licensed, bonded, and insured, or the one who says, "Hey, if you're not satisfied with our work, then we'll give you 100% of your money back. Oh, and by the way, here's over 1,000 testimonials, including several dozen from your neighbors describing their experience with us." I mean, come on. This is what we call, "A no brainer."

Other unique selling propositions are the code of ethics that I described earlier in this marketing program, and true same day service. True same day service implies that many companies offer same day service, but they really don't provide it. That's the reality of their industry. Most companies who offer same day service usually can't provide it, especially in peak seasons like winter and summer. The full page dedicated to sales and new systems has a headline that states, "Five secrets contractors don't want you to know." It then goes onto describe how you probably need a new furnace if yours is over 11 years old, and what five things you need to know before you make an investment in a new system.

Use Videos That EXPLAIN

We then make an offer to go to their website to watch their free series of energy saving videos, and to download the free report entitled, "The homeowners guide to hiring service contractors. How to make sure you never suffer by hiring the wrong company." This special report has proved to be one of the most valuable tools in their arsenal. In it we describe the most common problems that people have with service contractors, and how to avoid them. Of course the only company that ensures that clients avoid these problems is our company, Express Heating and Cooling. Of course the report does a great job of highlighting the unique selling propositions of my client, that literally nobody else can offer.

For example, "Are you aware of the fact that it's absolutely possible to have a lien put against your home simply because you hired the wrong heating and air conditioning contractor?" Not only is this true, but it actually happens more time than you'd ever want to believe. The reason for this is simple, if a contractor does not pay for their equipment up front before they install it in your home, a manufacturer of the ... order to receive payment. If this happens to you, you'll be forced to pay for your equipment twice. Now, the only way to ensure this does not happen to you is to work with a company that is a cash liquid company, meaning that they own every single piece of equipment that they install.

Strive for Exclusivity

Guess what? Our client happens to be the only contractor in the state who is a cash liquid company, and he's therefore literally the only one who can make this kind of claim to protect customers from having a lien put against their home. The report then gives homeowners this instruction, "To protect yourself, ask your contractor if they actually own the equipment they're installing in your house, or if they're using payment terms with their suppliers." You see how we're facilitating the decision making process by defining the criteria that prospects should look for in an HVAC contractor? You see how we're making people feel like they'd have to be completely insane to work with anybody else, no matter the price? Wait, there's more. This is going to get better.

We also developed a script for this report. Yes, it's available online to download for free, but we've also printed it out in full color on glossy stock with UV coating. It looks as good as the cover of National Geographic. Seriously. The printed copy is handed to customers when service technicians arrive at their front door, and the script is then recited. Now, put yourself in the prospect's shoes. Imagine you are Pete the proverbial prospect, or Pete's wife, and your furnace or air condition is broken and you call this company to come fix it. You're already skeptical and nervous, and then the technician shows up.

When he gets to the door he looks clean and professional, and then he recites this to you when you open the door. "Hello Mrs. Jones, my name is Jason with Express Heating and Cooling. We understand that a lot of people are skeptical of service contractors like us because of negative experiences that people have had in the past. In order to protect you from any future grief, we've prepared this homeowners guide to hiring service contractors. Once you've read the information in this guide, you'll be equipped enough knowledge to ensure you never have a bad experience with any contractor ever again. I want to go ahead and leave you with a copy of it for free."

The technician then hands the printed copy of the report to the customer. How do you think that changes the environment? What happens to the customer's confidence level? I mean it skyrockets. Think about it folks, how else do you think we get those thousands of testimonials? What do you think the customer is doing while the technician is working on their broken equipment? That's right, they're reading the special report, and having their confidence built even more. In fact, they're being convinced whether they realize it or not, that Express Heating and Cooling is the very best company of its kind, and they made the best decision possible when they chose them.

You Must Have Scripts!

Since the report is printed on such nice paper and it looks so nice and professional, they just don't throw it away. It sits around on their coffee table for friends and family to read when they come over. Of course that's just one script, we also have scripts for the customer service representatives that they recite when somebody calls for service, or when they call inquiring about a new system, or when they call in response to one of our ads.

You see, everything has to be scripted. You can't leave it to chance. This is the systematized sales process we're talking about. We need to have systems in place to ensure that as much as possible, our customers and prospects all have the same experience with us. Even the on hold message was custom scripted using the strategic messaging formula.

There's still a whole lot more to it.

We've created a brochure for technicians to leave to generate leads for the sales team. Again, we use the strategic messaging formula to create the content for the brochure.

We also have three different door hangers that were all developed using the strategic messaging formula, and that all have special offers with unique headlines. For example, one of the headlines says, "Invest $49 in a tune-up for your air conditioner, and I will guarantee you a 100% profit in writing." Other door hangers are placed on the doors of the five homes surrounding any other home that a service technician just serviced. The door hanger announces, "We've just serviced your neighbor's house, and we're confident that we can help you save money this year too!"

We also created magnets with special offers, and stickers with QR codes to place on furnaces and air conditioners. When the QR code is scanned on a smartphone, it automatically calls the company. Of course the phone number's there too, so if and when the customer has a problem with their furnace, our number is easy to find. Speaking of smartphones, we also developed a mobile website that is optimized for mobile phones with tap to call features, and other mobile specific content.

We also created over 15 radio ads using the strategic messaging formula, and over 30 postcards and sales letter to generate new business, especially during spring and fall when repair calls slow down.

Once leads come in to the sales team, we developed what has to be the most advanced sales system in the industry. It's probably one of the most advanced sales system in any industry. In short we created a complete sales presentation with customized graphics, and a custom developed sales script. When I say customized graphics, I mean every single page of this sales presentation was custom designed with my clients branding and imaging. It included pictures of a poor installation compared to a good one. What to look for, and what to avoid. Including actual pictures of competitor's vans and trucks with their company names Photo-shopped out and replaced with generic names, but the customer gets the point.

We then walk the customer through the entire process of what to look for in a furnace or air conditioning system. We have a system developed that allows our sales person to take some quick measurements of the home, and determine exactly how much money they're paying down to the penny per hour. The calculations are compared with their actual bills, and were always right on target. This allows the sales person to give a reasonable estimate of how much money they can save on energy expenses by getting a new system.

Yes, it gets even better.

See, every other contractor will talk how they are the authorized dealers of name brand companies like Drain, or Carrier, or York, or Amana, or Linux, or whoever. Guess what? Most of those companies don't offer exclusive dealerships, and most of the products are not that much better than the next one anyway. In fact, most of the products are all the same and they come from the same manufacturer. One day Jim showed me one of his major suppliers actually sends him four different stickers in every box with the furnace, so he can choose what company he wants to put on the equipment. It's all the same equipment from the same manufacturer, they just choose the sticker to put on there.

When I saw that I asked Jim, "Hey, why don't you just white label the product? This way you can be exclusive and have an additional USB." Jim say he'd love to but then asked, "Do you know how much trouble it is to create a complete company and product line, complete with all the marketing of website and everything else just to have a white label?" I could tell just thinking about it was exhausting to him. I responded, "What do you think you hired us for? We'll have that white label company up and running in no time." I then sent him five or six different names for a white label company. He chose one, we'll call it, "Super Tech." Then we developed a logo, a website, and some brochures, and we were off to the races.

Then at the end of the sales presentation, the sales person describes how Express Heating and Cooling is the exclusive dealer for Super Tech heating and air systems, and how we have the best warranties in the business. Which is true, because our client is providing the warranty themselves. See, we have up to a 30-year warranty on our top of the line equipment. What's hilarious is that these name brand companies like Carrier, York, Drain, and Amana have spent decades developing their brand, and in 30 minutes we convinced prospects that our white label company, Super Tech, is the leader in the industry and the standard by which all others should be judged because of our systematized sales process.

It's become so frustrating to competitors, that some of them have actually inquired on our Super Tech website about how to become dealers. They have no idea that Super Tech is a white labeled product, and that their inquiries are coming to their competitor, Express Heating and Cooling. True story. Then the sales person pulls out custom developed pre-printed pricing manuals in full color glossy stock. These are beautifully designed pricing manuals that look like fancy brochures, but they're actually price guides. Now, compare this to everyone else in the industry who brings out black and white quotes with blank lines, where they manually write down quotes. I mean it's pitiful. How can you have any confidence that you're getting the best price when they're manually writing down the pricing on each quote? As a business, how are you not shooting yourself in the foot when you don't standardize your pricing? You're basically beginning the client to ask you for a lower price, thereby lowering your profits.

Now, understand this was a major undertaking. In addition to all the work already put into developing the sales system, we had to create pricing manuals for four different product levels, each with four different sizes, and in five different system types. The result was that we had to create special pricing manuals for over 40 different HVAC systems. Then we had to develop a filing system so that once the sales person had determined the right size unit for the prospects home, he could reach into his folder and pull out just three of those pricing manuals. A good, better, or best system, and start with the best for the prospect. The prices are pre-printed so there's no question about pricing integrity. If the price is too high, the customer can drop down to the next product level as opposed to discounting. You know, go down from best to better, and, if necessary, down from better to merely good.

Every Step Is Choreographed in Advance

The prices are negotiated, they're pre-printed and the quality of the material is so professional that nobody assumes they can deviate from those prices. Of course there's actually more details into how we created the system, and every step of the development process is multi-tiered, and takes a lot of energy and effort to ensure that we're maximizing the results at every step along the way. What was the end results of implementing a systematized sales process? Well, starting the first week we implemented the sales system, the sales presentation went from being an average of 3 hours long, to 45 minutes long. Closing ratios were up by over 30%, and margins were up by over 11%. We've had to double the size of the sales force. In fact, after one year of implementing a complete marketing program, along with systematized sales processes like I just described, Express Heating and Cooling has had to hire nearly 50 new employees. They've had record sales continuously each quarter, they've become the number one company in their industry, and it's actually the largest contractor in our state.

Extremely Powerful Program!

I don't mean the largest HVAC contractor, but the largest contractor period. They're actually now one of the top 50 HVAC contractors in America, and they're going to break 8 figures in revenue, which is an amazing feat in their industry. In short, in about a year's time they have achieved total dominance. Now I know what you might be thinking. You're probably thinking, "Yeah, those are great results, but look at how much work you had to do to get there." Yeah exactly, that's the point. If you want to be number one, if you want to reach a place of total dominance, there are no shortcuts my friend. You have to do the work that I described here. Look, our program is not called the, "Wimpy Marketing Program," the, "Average Marketing Program," or the, "Kind of Cool Marketing Program."

No, it's called the, Power Marketing Program. You know why? It is truly power, and it works. It really only applies to businesses who have guts and courage. In other words, businesses and business owners who are powerful enough to take this information and implement it. This marketing program is called, "Total Dominance," for a reason. You see, when you take the effort and make the investments we've described on this marketing program, superior results are inevitable. You can and should absolutely rise to total dominance in your industry and your market sector if you follow the instructions we've given you in this program.

We've used several different examples and case studies from different industries on this program, so you can see how this scientific approach works in all industries since it's based on human nature. There are no exceptions to this rule. Regardless of your industry, no matter what you sell, or where you sell, whether locally, regionally, nationally, and/or internationally and who you sell to, consumers or business to business, as long as you're selling to humans, this system will work, period.

Now, as you are aware there is a fifth step in the Power Marketing Program. That step is having a professionalized image, now, for sake of time I'm not going to review this step in detail. The point here is simple and obvious. If you want to dominate you must always act and look like the consignment professional. A professionalized image directly impacts the amount of confidence your prospects have in you. Remember what you learned earlier, the amount of money someone's willing to give you is directly proportional to the amount of confidence they have in your ability to provide them with the goods and services that they want or need. Just remember, in everything you do, look like a professional. Act like a professional, and be a professional. The market deserves it. Consider it your duty.

Well I hope you've enjoyed the strategies and tactics outlined in this book. I know I covered a lot with you. I talked about the two most common marketing mistakes that businesses are making. I talked about eliminating platitudes and implementing a complete marketing system. I talked about the importance of business innovation, and we talked in relative detail about how the strategic messaging formula can allow you to craft messages that cut through a cluttered marketplace, and cause your prospects and customers to draw the conclusion that they'd have to be completely insane to work with anybody else but you, no matter the price.

We also gave you plenty of examples and case studies along the way. Here's the shocking part; believe it or not, what you've learned is literally just the tip of the iceberg. Implementing the complete Power of Marketing program in its entirety covers every facet of a company's marketing place. To find out more you're going to have to connect with a certified Power of Marketing consultant, or attend one of our live seminars. To find a certified Power of Marketing consultant nearest you, visit our website at PowerMarketingConsultants.com.

I am certainly confident that by now you've learned plenty about marketing your business properly. I hope you can understand now why we have titled this program, "Total Dominance, how to become the number one company in your industry using the Power of Marketing program." The good news is that now you've learned what it takes to do marketing the right way. The bad news is that for most people, even though they learned how to change their marketing, they often don't do it. There's typically one of two reasons for this.

Number one, because the old way, the wrong way of doing marketing is so ingrained on their mind that they simply can't get out of that mode of thinking, and they're unable to execute the power of marketing program. Hey, old habits die hard.

Number two, believe it or not some people are so hurt and offended that we've not only told them that they've done something wrong, but actually proved it, and demonstrated it through our various evaluations like you learned about in this program that they simply won't change because to do so would be to admit error. I know that sounds ridiculous, but I'm telling you that many people's egos are so fragile that they would rather lose money and destroy their own companies profit potential, than admit that they've been doing marketing wrong. It's just another facet of human nature.

Look, I'm not intending to hurt anybody's feelings. On the contrary, I'm here to help you. Sometimes, however, in order to be helped, you need to be given a healthy dose of the truth. In marketing, my friend, the truth will set your profits free. Think about it, if I can increase your company's profits from five to 5,000% wouldn't you consider that helpful? What would it mean to you personally if you could double or triple your company's bottom line this year? What would it mean to you personally if you could afford to hire additional employees and provide more income for your existing employees? How would you feel if you knew that you were the number one company in your industry, and your business was the standard by which all others were judged?

Think about it, marketing has the potential to bring all those feelings into reality. I can tell you that the most fulfilling part of my job is going on site to my customers' offices and seeing the new employees that they've had to hire since we've been working with them, and helping them grow their companies. There's nothing more rewarding than that, really.

From here you're probably wondering what the next step is. Well there are really three main options at this point.

One, perhaps you've learned enough from reading this book that you don't need any more help. That is possible. If so, fantastic. I'm sure you'll consider the purchase of this book money well spent.

A second and highly popular option is to attend one of my live seminars. These seminars are held periodically throughout the year. You can find the dates on my website.

Lastly, some of you may want to engage me personally in a one on one consultative relationship for your business. Contact my office for details. I would love to talk with you and see if we are a good fit to work together. The Power Marketing consultants network is the number one marketing network in the world, made up of professionals around the world who have all been trained to execute and implement the Power of Marketing program that you've learned about here, and who all share resources to ensure that we are maximizing our customers return on investment.

We have regular mastermind sessions and weekly ad reviews, where network consultants get feedback from senior level consultants, including myself. Yes, if you engage a certified Power Marketing consultant, I personally will more than likely review the content that is developed for your own marketing system, and help design it so that you get the best results possible. Additionally, we have developed a program for direct consulting clients called the, "Virtual Marketing Department." The concept is simple. In short you would simply be outsourcing your marketing needs to one of our network consultants at just a fraction of what it would cost to hire a marketing director. A marketing director who would more than likely do your marketing all wrong anyways, like you've learned about in this program.

With the Virtual Marketing Department, you would pay the consultant a monthly retainer fee, like you would to a lawyer. Along with a participation fee based on your business growth. The specific fees and participation percentage can be determined after the initial consultation. As we discussed in the opening part of this marketing program, we need to highlight the fact that we're really not looking to work with every business out there. In fact, we can actually only offer the Virtual Marketing Department service to one company in any industry, in any market. Either you, or your competitor. Whoever gets to us first.

I'm looking to work with businesses that really want to be the best that they can be. People who have such a passion for their customers, and doing things the right way that they'll do whatever it takes to get good enough to deserve all the business. I'm looking for people who can't stand at the thought of a customer doing business with a competitor. If you strive for that kind of excellence, then reach out and contact me at mikeloganmarketing.com. I want to thank you again for investing in my book.

Rich Contractors ... utilize well designed marketing and sales systems to dominate the competition.

Poor Contractors ... you should know the answer by now.

ABOUT THE AUTHOR

Mike was born and raised in California; he has attended several universities and holds two college degrees. For over 40 years, Mike has been in the swimming pool design and construction industry, and he holds three Contractor's Licenses. Pool builder C-53, Landscape contractor C-27 and Concrete contractor C-8. Mike has won numerous international Design Awards for his unique and creative pools that he has built over the years. His company, Logan Pools Inc., was named one of the top 100 pool companies in the country and, for over 10 years, was voted Best Pool Builder in Brentwood CA. Mike is a Public Speaker and #1 Best Selling Author on the topics of Marketing, Sales and Leadership. To arrange for a FREE 30 minute telephone consultation contact Mike via email at:

Mike@loganpools.com

www.ingramcontent.com/pod-product-compliance
Lightning Source LLC
Chambersburg PA
CBHW050208230526
45470CB00001B/284